Top Agent

"If you do what you've always done, you'll get what you've always gotten."

—**Tony Robbins**

Top Agent

Stories of Success from Industry-Leading Real Estate Professionals

Volume One

Keith Dougherty

Florida

Top Agent

Copyright © 2016 Keith Dougherty

All rights reserved.

XMS Publishing

1391 NW St. Lucie West Blvd, Suite 247

Port St. Lucie, FL 34986

This publication is designed to provide accurate and authoritative information regarding the subject matter covered. It is sold with the understanding that the publisher is not engaged in rendering legal, accounting, medical, or other professional services.

The information and opinions presented in this book are intended for educational purposes only. Any income claims or results discussed in this book are not typical and they are for example only.

ISBN-10: 0692702083
ISBN-13: 978-0692702086

Published in the United States of America

"Limitations live only in our minds. But if we use our imaginations, our possibilities become limitless." –Jamie Paolinetti

Dedication

This book is dedicated to every child out there that is fighting a life-threatening illness. Our thoughts and prayers are with you every day. Never give up and always keep fighting.

Table of Contents

Introduction

"Whatever the mind of man can conceive and believe,
it can achieve." – Napoleon Hill

Welcome to Top Agent. One day, I had a notion. I said to myself, "Why don't you host your own radio show." Little did I know that I would focus solely on successful people in real estate. My show first started on Business Innovators Magazine and has now grown to Real Estate Innovators Radio (http://realestateinnovatorsradio.com/). If you are an agent reading this and you want to be considered for the show, just go to our site and submit a request to be interviewed. Please be patient, as our guest list has grown significantly.

Okay, now back to my story of how this book came to life. I was interviewing and meeting great people, many of whom you will meet in this book. They are top agents, brokers, and business owners. But the most important thing is that they are real people, no matter how much success they had. The common trait you will see they all share is that they truly care about other people. They care about finding out what people need and helping people fill that need.

So, after my 19th show, I said to myself, "You need to share these stories of success with everyone." And so Top Agent was born.

Now, to make it even better, all of the contributors to this book and I have decided to donate 100% of the retail royalties to charity, specifically St. Jude Children's Research Hospital. According to their website, "St. Jude is leading the way the world understands, treats and defeats childhood cancer and other life-threatening diseases."

If you would like to make a donation and support this great charity to help kids, you can visit: stjude.org

Top Agent Carolyn Moriarty

Carolyn Moriarty is the founder of Carolyn Moriarty and Company, based out of Altamonte Springs, Florida. Among her many accomplishments in real estate, she quickly rose to the top and in only seven years was awarded the most prestigious RE/MAX Lifetime Achievement Award.

Not only that, she has sold over one hundred million dollars plus in volume and was voted Best Client Satisfaction from 2008 to 2015. She was also featured in Orlando Home Buyer Magazine and Top Agent Magazine and she was Woman of the Year for the National Association of Professional Women.

What led you to real estate? Was it something you always knew you wanted to do?

I was in a sink or swim situation. I was a single mother. I had to raise my two children alone and I had to find something I knew would be rewarding and provided a good payoff for the hours of time I worked versus working for someone in an 8 to 5 job. I thought that real estate would be the best way to go because I had previously worked for an investment firm wherein they took over mortgages subject to foreclosures and similar legal action. This was back in the day.

Then the people that owned the house would give the house over to the investor, who would keep up the mortgage payments. They would rent out the house or sell it and the customer they bought the home from would be free and clear from their liabilities and obligations. I have a lot of research on the bank-owned or foreclosure side of it. When I left that company, I was only making 60 thousand dollars a year, which was not enough to support my two children. I decided to go into real estate.

When I was married back in 1999 I got my real estate license, but never utilized the license until about nine years ago, after I left the investment firm. I got into it full-force, putting in long hours. I had a can-do attitude, very aggressive, worked night and day. It was flexible. I could take my children to functions and events they needed to go to, but then work the business at night when they were sleeping. I could have a versatile schedule where I could be there for them, but also be able to make a decent living.

I give 100% in everything I do. I have to have meaning and purpose and I have to be very, very, very transparent and honest. I'm a black and white kind of person. If it works, it works. If it doesn't, it doesn't. My motto is if option A doesn't work, go to option B. If option B doesn't work, find option C.

What personal attributes, traits, or qualities do you think have contributed the most to your success and how did you develop these?

One of the big things that affected me was that I was raised without a mother. My father raised me. He had great work ethic. I was never scared of hard work and long hours. Believe me, in this business, it takes dedication, long hours, but more importantly, honesty and transparency.

Can you give a specific example of how your traits have played a role in your path toward success?

Absolutely. I started out with RE/MAX in 2008. I think it was June of 2008. That was with RE/MAX Select. I did everything that I could there until I transitioned over to RE/MAX Assured. I was always the top agent when I was with RE/MAX Select. In the first six months, I reached the 100% Club in real estate, which is earning 100 thousand dollars' gross commission. Then every year after that, I made the Chairman Club, which is 250 thousand dollars' gross commission. Then I switched over to another RE/MAX office, which was RE/MAX Assured.

In my seven years of being with RE/MAX, I have always been number one. At the office, I was always number one. I was running and gunning and just putting in the time to get the most I could because I wanted to be the best that I could be in the industry. After I had achieved everything in only seven years with RE/MAX, which was the Lifetime Achievement Award, I branched out on my own. Now, I have to to break that down for you in terms of the Lifetime Achievement Award; that was three million gross commission sales in only seven years and it takes most people a substantial amount of time to achieve that.

My vision was to build a brokerage based on morals and ethics, but more importantly, teaching new agents how to be successful. I know what it feels like to be in a situation in which I need help, and because of that, I try to reach out to people who are in the same situation or the same dynamics I had been faced with. I strive to give them one-on-one, hands-on training and help them learn the most important thing – that your word is your bond and your word means more than any green dollar bill.

Now that I have agents in my brokerage, I'm physically holding their hands and taking them to listing appointments, helping them on sales calls, and doing mock calls with them. I'll get on the phone with them. They'll be on the other line. I'll handle the transactions for it because I understand it from start to finish. That's where I'm achieving my joy now, in reaching out and giving someone that's in the same situation that I was in the opportunity, but allowing them to gain hands-on experience.

I have eight agents, as we speak, in my brokerage. I have agents call me at 2:00 in the morning and say, "Hey, I just submitted a contract. Can you look over it and make sure I did it right?" So I get up at 2:00 in the morning. I look over the contract and I go, "You need to change this, this, this, this." You always have to protect your customer. They make the changes. I go back to bed, wake up the next morning, and do it again.

What were some of the major adversities and trials you had to overcome to achieve your goals?

Long hours; making sure you have a good accountant; making sure that if you're producing and making a lot of money, you meet with your accountant to make sure your corporation is set up correctly, whether it be an S corporation or a C corporation. Make sure that you have an attorney on standby in case you have any legal issues and you need to ask them for legal advice. My reputation is flawless. Have I been threatened to be sued? Yes, on two or three occasions, but I have a flawless reputation.

My word is my bond and it means more to me than any green dollar bill, but I have to do it with purpose and meaning. Just like the company name, I created it. The business cards are hearts. They're actual physical two-fold hearts. The C of my name, Carolyn, the M of my name, Moriarty, put together makes a heart, *the* heart, the heart of the home.

That's what I want to convey to people, that we are the heart of your home. We want to make sure that every decision that's made and each and every transaction comes from the heart and that it's very transparent and honest.

I think in every business there are roadblocks. I guess, especially when you're starting your own brokerage, it's exciting, and on the other hand, it's scary. You just have to have endurance. Your attitude matters. You have to wake up in the morning and say, "It's going to be a great day." It's your positive energy. Yeah, there's a lot of negativity and a lot of unethical practices in the industry, but you have to rise above that. If you're experienced enough, you want to see through that.

The way I work is, if I don't get the answers or I feel that the transaction is not transparent or it feels like something's not being disclosed, I dig deeper until I reach my comfort level. This is both for me as the broker and for either the seller or the buyer. There's a lot of shady stuff in the real estate industry. There are a lot of unethical practices. If you're a newbie, we take the oath of being a REALTOR®: to disclose all know facts that materially affect the value of the property, to account for all funds, and to be honest in everything you say and do.

When I took that oath, I took it to heart. I think dishonesty and hiding information or not disclosing information would be a huge roadblock for me.

What kept you going despite these obstacles? Why didn't you give up?

I want to make sure I get the best deal and do the best thing for the customer. I am assuming that it's just my work ethic and the way I was raised. I want to make sure that the customer is protected, whether it be a buyer or seller. I will say, "You know what? I don't know that this is correct. I think we need to do some further research. I think we need to go to the county. We need to go to the city. There's just something that's not sitting right here with me." Then it's up to the customer at that time, once the information is presented, whether they want to proceed or whether they want to withdraw.

I give them my professional opinion and what I feel. Then ultimately it's up to the customer, but at least I know I've done the right thing by digging deeper and gathering additional information so they can make an informed, intelligent decision that they're comfortable with.

What is your vision for your business over the next five years?

I hope to be one of the largest brokerages in Central Florida, but I want to build a brokerage where agents want to stay, where they don't want to leave, where they don't want to get my knowledge and then go with some other brokerage. I might even have another location. I just purchased my commercial building in November and I have eight agents. I left RE/MAX in May of last year. I don't know what the future holds. It's in God's hands.

I just know I'm going to continue doing what I do and I'm going to surround myself with people that are like-minded and have the same morals and ethics as I do. I want people that are honest and transparent and that disclose and research any and every part of the transaction that's needed for the benefit of the customer. As long as I surround myself with people like myself, I know we will have tremendous growth.

What do you feel is the best way you market yourself as a real estate professional for continual growth?

My philosophy is once I have a customer, I have that customer for life. I don't want to sell an individual a house or list their house and lose them as a customer. My philosophy is I do the very absolute best job that I can for the customer, and then when they buy a new house, they refer me out to all of their friends and family. I've got tons of people that won't use anybody else but me because they know how I work. I've got tons of customers. At my grand opening of my brokerage, I had 150 people plus show up for it.

What do you think is the biggest misconception/myth that people have about working with real estate agents?

When starting out as a new agent, it seems that a lot of brokerages always tell you to go to your sphere of influence. Yeah, you can go to your sphere of influence, but if you don't have one, then what? I know when I got started with RE/MAX, no one gave me the individualized training I'm providing to my agents. I have people in different areas of the industry, title companies, mortgage companies, that come into my brokerage to train my agents.

I want my agents to know the right and the wrong way to do things. Again, I know I always focus on honesty and transparency. If you're out for a quick dollar bill and you think you're going to get rich quick in real estate, you're in the wrong industry. You're doing it for the wrong reasons. I get the most joy when I see a person try so hard because they want a house. I get them qualified with a mortgage broker. We find them a house and that is the biggest, most rewarding experience, when I can get them into a home that they thought they could never own.

I am a walking testimony. It's dedication. It's a lot of hard work. It's long hours. You get out of it what you put into it. I'm constantly trying to keep up with the technology, to be on the next thing when it comes to marketing. Whatever it takes, I'm constantly adapting to meet my customers where they are. We've got to keep up because everything is constantly changing. We should be as knowledgeable as possible in every aspect of real estate. If you are asked, "How much are my closing costs going to be? How much am I going to have to come to the table with?" you know how to tell them. There are formulas for that.

If you were to get a call from a family member in another state wanting to sell their home, what advice would you give them about selecting an agent who can best serve their needs?

What I do is research that particular state and find the best top-producing agent. I would interview the agent myself. I advise them of my customer's particular situation and their home. Then I fill out a referral fee so I get a 25% referral fee when they sell that home. In exchange for that, I want them to keep me in the loop of the transaction, of the showing. I don't work in that state, but I have my hand on the pulse and I'm guiding my customer accordingly.

I want to look at their track record and how many sales they have made and how many years they've been in the industry. Real estate changes each and every day. The laws are constantly changing. What you want to look for are statistics. You want to look for reviews. You want to search for them online. If you can, get a recommendation from someone that you know, maybe even two, then interview the agents to see which one your customer might click with.

How can someone who needs a real estate agent find out more about you and how you can help?

They can go to my web-site, CarolynMoriarty.com, or they can reach me at 407-252-5457. If you would prefer e-mail, you can reach me here: Carolyn@CarolynMoriarty.com.

Top Agent Henrik Alaverdyan

Henrik specializes in serving clients who are looking to buy or sell property in Los Angeles and the surrounding cities. He has a comprehensive understanding of the market and skillful and strategic pricing and marketing. He believes he is not Number One. His clients are. It's all about the client and their best interests.

Plain and simple, Henrik helps people every step of the way when purchasing or selling homes, providing professional and trustworthy service. No hype, no fluff, straightforward and experienced. Henrik is here to stay.

What led you into real estate? Was it something you knew you always wanted to do or did you just stumble into it?

What led me to real estate was the fact that I knew I am a people person. I want to help families make the right choice with what is likely one of the biggest financial decisions they'll have to make in their life. I had a couple of career paths in front of me from which to choose, but in the end, I feel that I have made the right decision. I love what I do and I am good at it. What more can one ask of their career choice?

What personal attributes, traits, or qualities do you think have contributed the most to your success and how do you think you developed those?

Ever since I was young, my parents always involved me in sports. I started playing basketball at age four and continued until I was about 16. On almost every team I played, I was the team captain. I helped lead the team to victory. After that, I joined mixed martial arts.

I know it may sound silly since these are just sports, but the time, dedication, discipline, and hard work needed to succeed really helped me create great work ethics, for which I am now known. A few years later, here I am helping families turn their dreams into reality and making sure that the decisions they make are educated ones.

Do you think you could give some specific examples of when these traits have played a role in your path toward success, especially when it's come to real estate?

Absolutely. It seems that nowadays public opinion is that real estate is easy money, but truth be told, if you're doing it right, it's anything but easy. Anyone with a license can submit an offer or list a property, but knowing what is in your client's best interest and fighting for it, it is not a given and it's not easy.

14

My job is not to submit an offer or list a property. My job is to do what I just mentioned and fight for my clients. I've had many situations where clients have been in love with the property, and just like a doctor delivering bad news, I have to tell my clients, "This isn't the one. This will cause you big problems down the line." Pretty much, their heart breaks. They're in love with the property. Conversely, I've had the situation when listing a property for sale where the buyers are trying to bully my client into taking a bad deal and I have to fight with the other agent to get favorable terms for my seller. That strength and ability to overcome obstacles I can directly attribute to my past experiences.

There's a reason why the client hires me and it's my job to guide them and lead them to the right decisions. I don't want them to end up in a deal where, later on down the road, they're going to be pretty much in a bad situation.

What are some of the major adversities or trials you've had to overcome to achieve your goals?

My parents supported me when I first started out on this path. I wasn't born with a silver spoon in my mouth, so everything that I have, I have had to work for. Like many of the top agents around town, there was a lot of sacrifice when I first started out, missing holidays with my family, not being with friends in various activities. Being essentially self-employed, I've had to invest everything I make back into my career.

I have no regrets. Every sacrifice I made was for my clients and for my career and I stand by it. Additionally, I am young and earning the respect of my colleagues and the trust of my clients was not the easiest task. I had to prove myself at every juncture, but looking back at it now, those tests made me better.

What kept you going, despite these obstacles? Why didn't you give up?

It's simple. I have a vision. In order to succeed, you need to have a vision. You need to set goals and have a plan and work towards that plan every single day. No matter how tired you are, you don't stop. I have the mentality where I don't stop when I'm tired. I stop when I'm done. People my age would go party, clubbing, and whatnot, but I was in my office thinking of ways to better serve my clients and to market myself uniquely because of so much competition. You can't just expect things to happen without putting any effort or work into it.

What is your vision for your career for the next five years?

I love this question. I want to build my own empire within the next five years. What better way than to follow in the footsteps of the well-known entrepreneurs that have already built their empire? Barbara Corcoran, from Shark Tank, built her empire with real estate. I also look up to Dave Ramsey, Mark Cuban, Daymond John, and many more wonderful leaders.

What do you feel is the best way you market yourself as a real estate professional for continued growth?

Going back, giving the highest level of customer service to all clients as a real estate professional for continued growth is the best way to go. It doesn't matter for me if the client is looking for a $200,000 house or a $2 million house. The service must stay the same. You can market all you want and try all the different marketing techniques, but if you're not listening to your clients and providing them with what they need, they won't be around too long.

At the moment, most of my business comes from referrals. For me, that's the highest level of appreciation from clients. That just means I did something right and that's the best way to market yourself in the business that I'm in when looking for continual growth.

I'm in the business of making people more money. With buying a house, I'm the one that takes away the stress that comes with the process of buying or selling. I make sure my clients are fully satisfied, just like I said, regardless of whether they're buying a $200,000 house or a $2 million house. Customer service must stay the same.

What do you think is the biggest misconception/myth that people actually have about working with a real estate agent?

There are plenty of myths when it comes to working with a real estate agent. The biggest myth people have is the less commission you pay to sell, the more you make. This is from the seller's point of view. Discount brokers love to spread this myth. They claim to save sellers money by charging less. The truth is agents who are top producers and excel in this business do not discount services, simply because they don't have to. They know what their value is. They know what their worth is and they know what they can bring to the table at the end of the day.

I know that I work countless hours and spend my own money drawing in the widest audience of buyers possible, which results in a bidding war. I also know when those offers come in I am going to be able to get them higher. In short, I know that what I put into it my sellers get out of it and that what I charge to do this comes back in a higher final sales price.

Another myth is agents will say anything just to make a sale happen. Yes, there are agents who will say and do anything to make a sale happen, but at the same time it's unfair to look at every agent the same way. Before working with the agent you choose, it's best to do your homework, ask questions, and always check for reviews from previous clients. All you have to do is go on the Web and search the agent. There's Zillow and other Websites that provide testimonials.

I believe the top-producing agents who carry a great reputation in this business and practice real estate honestly and truthfully are very careful to uphold the client's trust.

If you were to get a call from a family member in another state wanting to sell their home, what advice would you give them about selecting an agent who can best serve their needs?

There is Top Agent magazine. There's a Website, Top Agent, where you can search for the top-producing agents and where they have good reputation. You can go on the Web. Before you hire an agent, you really need to sit down and ask these agents questions and make sure you pretty much get their sales record. Their reviews are Number One because those are real people that worked with those agents.

I come across great reviews for some agents and I come across reviews that are very bad. You have to service your client in a way that ensures when they're reviewing you, they're going to be all over the Web with positive comments. You want to make sure you really get that good review and testimonial from your client to generate more business. Before someone hires you, I believe they search the Web before even giving you a call. It's really important to have that online presence.

That's key in the business and that's why I personally make sure I always listen to my clients first. I make sure of what they're looking for and then I go into action mode and deliver what they want.

How can someone who needs a real estate agent find out more about you and how you can help?

Very, very easily. Call me at 818-731-4649 or visit me online at henriksells.com. I'm not one of those agents that you call and will not respond for days or even weeks. I'm always on top of my business. I'm in the business of making people more money, just like I said, and taking away the stress that comes with buying or selling a property.

I also have been published as a top agent in California in Top Agent magazine. You can find me on the web if you search my name and the article will also come up. I have numerous personal websites that make it easy for my clients to have access to me and any future client to gain more information about me.

I want to thank my parents, who have supported me day in and day out. Without their support, I wouldn't be where I am right now. I would love to thank my past and present clients for all the trust they have in my services, as they have received and are continuing to receive Top Notch Real Estate Services. Last, but not least, I want to thank John Hart Real Estate and my broker, Harout Keuroghlian, for all their support. It's very important for a broker and an agent to have a strong relationship and I feel that he's not just my broker; he's my partner. He's always there for me when I need something and what better brokerage to be a part of than one in which you feel like your broker is your partner.

Top Agent Jonathan Alexander

Jonathan Alexander is with the J Alexander Real Estate Group with Keller Williams, based out of Boca Raton, Florida.

Among his many accomplishments, he's the founder and Lead Listing Specialist for the J Alexander Real Estate Group. He entered into real estate in 2005. Since then he's, grown the J Alexander Group exponentially to become one of the preeminent real estate teams in South Florida, helping over 500 families buy and sell real estate in south Florida.

Jonathan is currently ranked in the top 1% of all REALTORS® in South Florida. Jonathan is known as one of the top listing agents in Palm Beach and Broward counties, providing a cutting-edge marketing plan and being at the forefront of technology, which gives his clients an unfair advantage. He was also featured on the cover of Top Agent Magazine and interviewed by Business Innovators Magazine, which can be heard on iTunes and highlights his commitment to excellence.

What led you to real estate? Was it something you always knew you wanted to do?

That's a great question. When I was 21 years old, I was introduced to real estate by my mother, who is a real estate investor. At that time, she was heavily investing in properties. She gave me the push I needed to move forward. Honestly, I've always been in sales, ever since I started working. Moving to real estate was just natural for me. I believe it was a perfect match.

What personal attributes, traits, or qualities have contributed the most to your success and how did you develop these?

I feel to be successful in real estate, or any business for that matter, you have to have a vision, drive, and determination. You have to have unwavering focus. You have to have the will to succeed at a high level.

As an entrepreneur, and I'm sure many can agree with me on this, it all starts with having goals, becoming the person that you envision at the top in your mind. I feel that you have to become that person first, before it happens.

You have to do the activity necessary to achieve the goals. You have to ask yourself (as I did), "What does a top producer do throughout the day?" What does their schedule look like to be able to achieve the numbers that I want to achieve?"

It's automatic in the sense that by becoming the person first, then doing the actions and activities day after day, you will end up having everything you've always wanted. That's been my approach since I started.

I already knew in my mind, even on day one when I started in real estate, that I was a top agent. I was a top agent in the making and eventually I would get to where I needed to be. It all has to do with your confidence and I've always been a very confident person.

Can you give a specific example of when these traits have played a role in your path toward success?

Throughout this journey, we've run into many obstacles, some bigger than others. There were a few times that the business could have sunk. Fortunately, we do have a great support system. I've surrounded myself with great people in all areas. I've had great advice.

I was able to remove myself from the situation in which we were involved and look in from outside the box. That gave me a lot of clarity and helped me think rationally about the situation.

Another trait that I feel is extremely important has been my relentlessness and my determination to succeed. Being in the real estate business, I've been told "No" thousands of times from all types of people. For example, there have been numerous times in which I was going for a listing and I was told "No."

I feel most people in that situation would just give up and move on to the next. But I would follow up with them monthly, or even weekly, until they decided to list with me. I knew I needed 7 "Nos." This is what they say; 7 "Nos" typically lead to a "Yes." A lot of it has to do with being persistent and continually asking for the business, especially when you know in your heart that you can do the job better than most. You can communicate better, you are more diligent, you have better marketing skills, and you're a better negotiator. That conviction has to be translated to the client unceasingly until they see it. I think that's been one of the key traits for helping us on the path toward success.

A lot of people are afraid of a "No." It's not that the person on the other side of the phone, or on the other side of the door, is telling *you* "No"; they're just saying "No" to the situation. It's extremely imperative for people to understand that they're just saying "No" to the situation and not to take it personally, but keep going.

What were some of the major adversities and trials you had to overcome to achieve your goals?

I would have to say the biggest obstacle that we've had has been growing our team with highly talented, motivated team players, if you will.

Initially, when you get into the business, you start off as a single agent. As the business starts to grow and you have more clients, you get busier and busier and you really can't handle it all.

If you don't take care of the situation, it ends up spiraling out of control. Eventually, either you end up burning out or your customer service quality drops significantly. I learned that the key to growing the business and having a life by design, not by default, is in having leverage.

Once I applied myself to learning all the necessary steps and started to hire talented and motivated team members, everything all of a sudden got better. That's why I truly believe that the team environment is extremely important.

Most agents end up doing everything themselves throughout their career. They miss out on a huge opportunity. They eventually either plateau or their customer service level drops and they lose repeat business.

I learned that by having a team, which is a newer concept in the real estate industry, we have specialists in every facet of the business. That way, our clients always receive A+ service. We make sure there is always someone available to assist them with their questions and needs.

What kept you going despite these obstacles? Why didn't you give up?

I would say the number one thing for not giving up is I've never been a quitter in life. I've always welcomed challenges. I've always taken them head on. I go back to the determination and the will to succeed that I had mentioned previously.

I'm the type of person who is very determined. Anybody that knows me will probably say the same thing. I know that failure is just not an option. I'm an extremely positive person and an optimist. I'm always looking at the positive side of things.

I know from every experience that there's no such thing as failure. To me, it's a learning experience. One of my favorite books is *Failing Forward* by John Maxwell, which is a great book. It talks about failing forward in life, learning from your mistakes and from your failures because that's how we get better.

I would say that's been the biggest thing for me, just knowing that things are always going to get better and not taking anything personally and focusing on the end result.

What is your vision for your career for the next five years?

Our five-year plan is to have a real estate business that is thriving even more than it is now, doing over $150 to $200 million a year in volume. We're also looking to expand our business into other markets, which includes capturing market share in other states, as well.

One of the most important goals, this is something new to me, is personally making ten people on our team millionaires. I find the joy is in the giving. Nothing would make me happier than helping them achieve all of their goals and dreams. Ultimately, it's confirming to them and myself that we both made a great decision to get into business together.

In regards to marketing our team and continuing to market our brand, I think we're very fortunate that we're at the forefront of technology in several different spaces. One of the things is being a younger, yet experienced agent. I'm 31 years old with 12 years of real estate experience and I truly believe technology drives us.

I'm also very big into branding. I feel it has to reflect who we are and what our business focus is. We're continually adding to the online space whether it be social media, search engine optimization, or online reviews. Those have been instrumental in our success. Nowadays, whenever we want a good restaurant, a good movie, or whatever else it may be, we look for reviews online.

We've been very fortunate. We've obtained several new clients from our reviews. They call us and already know who we are, what we do, what our clients say about us, and the experience they're going to receive by working with us. It's been a game changer for us.

What's the biggest misconception/myth that people have about working with a real estate agent?

I think, by far, the biggest misconception about working with a real estate agent is that we're all created equal and provide the same service.

The issue is that getting a real estate license is not hard. I'm sure you know that and our readers know that. That opens up the opportunity for people to get into our industry at really almost no cost. It's not hard to get into the real estate business.

There aren't many that take the business seriously, unfortunately, and they aren't looking to improve their level of service. When they do get a client, they drop the ball for one reason or another. Could be a lack of training or it could be just the lack of self-development. What happens is the client gets a bad taste of working with an agent and many times assumes we're all the same.

If I had to compare real estate agents, I would probably liken it to comparing restaurants. You're going to get exceptional service and amazing food at one restaurant and perhaps the one across the street is the complete opposite, maybe terrible food and crappy service.

That points me back to the question that you asked me before. I truly feel that's why client reviews are super important. That truly tells a story. I highly encourage anybody that's looking to buy/sell or even invest in real estate to look up your agent. Go online and look up the top agents with the best reviews and interview a few, then pick one. That would be my suggestion.

If you were to get a call from a family member in another state wanting to sell their home, what advice would you give them about selecting an agent who can best serve their needs?

I would suggest to them that they would have to hire somebody who has visibility online, somebody who is obviously a professional with a set marketing plan in place, who is going to do all the different things needed to market a home to get it sold. This is somebody who is going to communicate, which I feel is extremely important.

That's the biggest complaint that most sellers have is the lack of communication. Unfortunately, there are a lot of agents out there who will take a listing and the client never hears from them again.

I think it's imperative, again going back to the reviews, to find somebody that specializes in selling homes. Not all agents, as I said, are created equal. There are some agents that are better working with buyers. There are certain agents that are better working on the listing side. I think it's imperative that they find a listing specialist, somebody that does this at a very high level and can guide them in the right direction.

How can someone who needs a real estate agent find out more about you and how you can help?

If you're looking to buy, sell, or invest in real estate in South Florida, we would love to help. We cover Palm Beach, Broward, and Miami-Dade. If you want to find more information about us, or you want to read more about us, please go to www.jalexandergroup.com, or you can call us at 561-962-2865. We would love to set up a consultation and see how we can help you with all of your real estate goals.

Top Agent Jerome Smith

Jerome Smith is with Keller Williams, based out of Marietta, Georgia. Jerome has been in business for over 15 years, doing over 15 million in business last year alone. Jerome is a relocation and short-seller and is military-certified. He was also the number one agent for Keller Williams from 2001 to 2015 out of 250 agents. And in 2014, he was one of the Top 25 Georgia Real-estate Agents per Top Agent Magazine.

What led you to real estate? Was it something you always knew you wanted to do?

I got started when I came out of corporate America. I was a regional manager for Blockbuster video back in the day and I decided I want to do something new. I always knew I could sell things, but I didn't know if I could sell houses. So, I went to work for a builder and I started that way. Then a couple of years later, I decided I wanted to do my own thing and step out on my own. This gave me the opportunity to spend more time with my family and do the things I wanted to do, but it was also pretty demanding.

What personal attributes, traits, or qualities do you think have most contributed to your success and how do you think you developed those?

First off, I think when you say you're going to do something, you've got to do it and do it 100%. I'm straight up with my clients, and because of that, 90% of our business is referral business. What we try to do is to make sure the desires of the seller are met. We get everything they need to get them started in the home search and buying process. We strive to be a one-stop-shop agent. So, if they need something, we are there for them regardless of what they need and we will go the extra mile to get things done.

Can you give specific examples of when these traits have played a role in your path toward success?

Being honest with them, the client, right off the bat, and not giving them a line of bull. Your typical salesperson wants to chatter, chatter, chatter about things that sometimes don't mean a lot to the actual seller or the buyer. You want to stick to the facts and you need get to know the client. You pay attention to what they're saying and what they want to do and make sure you take care of them 100%. A lot of times, they don't know much about buying a house. We get a lot of first-time home buyers. So we make sure that we take extra care of those buyers, as well making sure they know we're there for them and we're going to take care of everything. We are going the extra mile and showing we care.

I think when it boils down to being a salesperson, if we show them we care, then they feel much more comfortable doing business with us and they refer their friends and family to us. Another thing we do is when someone wants to see a house we don't usually run out and meet them at the house. We try and bring them into the office and do a consultation. When we do this we find that we only have to take them out two or three times at most for them to buy a house. What we do during this consultation is we explain to them from start to finish what the process is going to be and we try to get to the point that we know exactly what their needs are.

There was a saying that "buyers are liars" because they don't know what they want. They buy something they said they weren't going to buy. Regardless, as you take them out you definitely let them do all the talking and ask them questions, such as, "What does that look like to you?" or, "What do you think about this feature or that one?" This is about getting to know their family's needs, really paying close attention to what they're saying. So, listening is key, absolutely.

What were some of the major adversities and trials you had to overcome to achieve your goals?

I love to talk. That's one thing that I had to really calm down so I could listen to what the buyers and sellers were saying. Sometimes, I can be straight to the point and I have to watch what I say because I may hurt somebody' feelings. For the most part, you really just have to take care of them and listen to what they're saying. For example, you may be dealing with a divorce situation, where one partner is happy and the other one is not. You have to make sure you're paying attention to the needs of both sides.

I'm selling families three or four or five houses during their lifetime and I'm selling their kids' houses at this point in my career. They were just babies when I first started, so it's definitely great. You should do what you say you're going to do and follow through and get everything done for them. The more you can do for them, the better off you'll be because it takes the stress off of them and then they'll get to a level of comfort where they'll do exactly what you ask them to do. So, it works out great.

I have two girls, so I've struggled to find a balance between being a good dad and a good agent. That's my biggest struggle in this whole career because everybody wants to look at properties when work and school are done for the day. When you've got a family that's the biggest struggle because they'll have soccer games and band competitions and all that stuff during those off hours. It takes a lot of commitment. It takes everybody in the household supporting the one that has to work on the weekends and holidays for the most part. That's probably been my biggest struggle, just trying to juggle that and be a good dad.

Another huge thing was the down market we hit in 2009 and 2010. I'll be honest. What you do at that point, when you know it's coming or you feel it's coming, is be sure you're aware of what are you going to do to get work.

You've got to cater to what the market is doing. That is exactly what we did, focusing on short-selling. It's what we did in 2011, 2012, and 2013, for the most part. Probably 80% of our business was short-sell business and that's how we survived. We figured out another way to draw up business because a lot of people weren't selling since their houses wouldn't appraise, the market was flat, and they were upside-down.

But one good thing a down market does is weed out the not-so-great agents. To me, it's a full-time job and that is how I treat it. One of the best pieces of advice I received was from my first broker. I said to her, "Well you know, Annie," I said, "I'll have to do this part-time. I've got a family. I don't want to jump the gun and be 100% commission right off the bat," and she says, "Well, never go to work expecting full-time pay for part-time work."

I sat there for a minute thinking about what she was saying and that's why I'm a full-time agent. This is what I do full-time; this is how I support my family because 80% of the agents don't work full-time. They either work part-time or they don't work at all. But it's hard to adjust to being 100% commission if you are the head of household. It's a struggle, but you do it. You figure out ways to make it work and then it works. If you do it 100% 40 or 50 hours a week, sometimes more than that, then you should make money, if you do what you say.

What kept you going despite these obstacles? Why didn't you give up?

Well, I have people who depend on me. I have two girls, one is fourteen and one is 22 and she's going to graduate from the University of Georgia. That's one reason that keeps me going. I'm doing it for them. That's my line, the answer to the question, "Why do you do what you do?" You've got to have a line, because if you don't have a line, then you're not going to do it. That's been my pushing point for the last fifteen years; I'm doing it for them. And they know it and they appreciate it. I have to have support them, being a single dad, so it's definitely why I keep going and doing what I'm doing. I want to make sure they have a decent life and they understand there are sacrifices to be made and they've made them for the most part. But it's worked out great. It's been a great career.

Typically, when I hire staff, the first couple days they're here, I make them come in and put a poster board up and I give them a homework assignment. I say, go home and think about your why. Put why you want to do this job and put pictures that represent why. It could be a vacation or it may be a special trip somewhere, whatever. That's going to be your motivation to get it done this year. It's going to be your goal, why you have to do what you need to do. And every time you look at that poster, it's going to give you more motivation because you did it, not me. It works out great.

What is your vision for your career for the next five years?

Well, my vision is that I don't have to work as much. I just started hiring a team. I have one buyer's agent, right now, and a part-time assistant, and I'm looking at hiring another buyer's agent. I guess, I want to work fewer hours, instead of trying to do it all. Not that I don't love what I do, but I'd love getting it down to like 50 hours a week instead of 70. My goal is to take a step back and be more the one who goes out and meets with people, the rainmaker so to speak, and not take care of so much of the actual day-to-day operations. I would like to go out and meet with builders and other people, to drum up more business for the team because that's going to keep them going. That's really what the team leader should be doing, going out and making sure that we have business that keeps everybody busy.

However, my main goal is to work less and take it easy for a while because I'm getting old. It's been fun, but working seventy hours a week is not that cool sometimes. You do what you got to do, but I think my goal is to work at least 10 or 15 fewer hours a week over the next few years, and who knows, I may retire. I'd like to get to level 7, which is what we call it at Keller Williams. When you get to level 7, you can walk away from the business and it runs itself. I'm about a level 3 right now, so I have some work to do over the next five years to get there, but we're going to do our best to get it done.

What do you feel is the best way you market yourself as a real estate professional for continual growth?

I'll be honest with you. I really haven't changed that much of my basic marketing methods since I started in this business. We stay in touch with our clients, we touch base physically, and they get something from us every quarter at least. We do a lot of drop-ins and take gifts to some of our top referral clients. They love my salsa for some reason, so I take them salsa, and we hand-deliver it to their house. We do stuff like that just to kind of stay at the forefront of their mind and that helps ensure they refer business to us. We also send out flower seeds every year. I get people calling me asking where their flower seeds are, where their calendars are, and stuff like that.

That's the key. It's just staying in touch with them and just making sure that you stay at the forefront of their minds. I think a lot of the time we don't have to speak for the business; we stay right there on them. I went on a listing appointment and the person had already met with three other agents. I asked him if any of them had asked for the listing and he said, "No." So, I ask him for the business. I said, "I'm here to do business. I've got the listing agreement here. I've got the signing and the car. I've got the lots ready to go." He said "Well, I'm fine with you because you're the only one that's asking for the business."

I think a lot of the time we don't ask for the business, which is crazy to me because that's why you're there. Staying in close contact, saying we'll market the house at the best level that we can. A lot of the time we'll even help them. We'll landscape the yard, get things going, and be the one-stop-shop agent. When we buy the house, sometimes I'll take everybody on the team and we'll walk the house, getting everybody on board. If it needs painting, we make sure the painters are there to give a quote. And we'll make sure the landscapers are there. Basically, I have a whole team that satisfies almost every need that each client has, but if you sit around and wait for the seller to call, these people will be waiting forever.

You do what you say you're going to do, be there, support them, and just take the ball and run with it, because a lot of the time the seller doesn't know what to do. It may be the second or third home they have sold, but they still don't know, but we do it every day. We try to take all that stress off of them and do what we say to get things done and make this easy on them. That's how we make this business work.

I think if you just listen to what the seller needs and wants, and if you can justify what you're saying and what you want them to do, they will clearly understand. I was at a house recently and we couldn't figure out why the house wasn't selling. It's great. They've done everything in the world to the house. So, I said something is wrong with the curb appeal; it has no curb appeal. I went over to Lowes and got flowers and I told them I'll be at your house at 6:30 tonight and I need everybody to help me because they had three kids to help us. I took flowers and shovels and stuff and we got out there and we started planting flowers and putting some curb appeal in there. They had two big bushes in front of the house and I said, "You need to take those bushes down." Well, you would have thought I said, "You need to chop your arm off or the arm of one of the kids," the way they looked at me. And I said, "No seriously, take them down because they're hiding the front porch." We took those down and the house looked like a totally different house.

You have to really justify what you're saying, what you're talking about doing, because they don't understand. The people at this house have been thrilled ever since the bushes came down and even the neighbors say, "Wow, your house looks different now that you've cut down the shrubs!"

You have to put a different hat on when you step in and a lot of times they'll challenge you. Sellers will challenge you, because they're overwhelmed with all the stuff they need to do, but if you take that burden off of them, it works out. I'll just tell them, "I'll tell you a lot of things. Some things you'll know; some things you won't know."

If they don't need to know, I'm not going to tell them. If they need to know, I'll tell them. If you do it that way, then it makes it ten times easier on people. I had another client call me the other day. On my listing appointment, the first thing out of her mouth when I got there was, "Stacy and Danny told us to do exactly what you say you're going to do and you could sell our house," and I said, "Well, we'll try." So a lot of times, as a referral, they're already set up for that. "If you do what he says, if you do what he tells you to do, you're going to sell your house." It works out pretty well.

What's the biggest misconception/myth that people have about working with a real estate agent?

Well, the funny thing is, people don't know what they're doing, that's what the funny thing is. The first thing an owner selling their own house will get with a potential buyer is, "Okay, you're not paying commission, so let me take 6% of the sales price, right off the bat." And then there is other issue that will come up; it's way too personal to try to sell your own house, when you've lived there and little Johnny's grown up there, little Susan's grown up there, and now you're trying to sell it. It's too personal. With an agent, the agent deals agent-to-agent and gets the job done because it's not really personal to them. It is, but it isn't.

A lot of times, probably 95% of the time, we get more money than they can get on their own when they are trying to sell it themselves because they're not educated and they don't do it every day. I had a client the other day who tried to negotiate his own deal without me, and when I got to talking to him, we ended up getting a cash offer from another buyer. Well, he had already negotiated this other deal on his own and didn't include me on it, so he shot himself in the foot. What happened was he struck a deal with a potential buyer who ended up not buying the property and the buyer we had who was going to pay cash for it walked because he wasn't going to wait. Buyers don't wait on a property. A lot of times, sellers think they know more than the agent does, but if you go in there and you can add value to what you're saying, they will be happy. They really don't want to sell it themselves, when it comes down to it.

They think they can save money, but if you can go in there and justify how you get things done and this is what you will do for them, they'll listen. It's a sales market right now and I've seen a lot more "For sale by owner" signs than I've seen in a long time. People are trying. However, another thing they run into is the issue of who they are letting into their house. They're taking phone calls directly. Then one day Johnny's going to show up, a psycho killer, and they're going to let him into the house while the husband is on a business trip. So, they let a stranger about whom they know nothing into the house and there's no way to track him down because there is no lock box and no known tracking system.

That's probably the number one thing that I would say for anybody who is thinking of selling their house themselves. Just think of the safety of your family, just by itself. Is it worth saving the 6%? Or is the extra 6% worth it to get the job done correctly, to watch over your house and make sure we know who is coming in and out of your house? People could be staking out your house and they will come back and rob you later. You never can tell. That's the biggest thing. I don't think that sellers actually think about that part of it. If you call the seller directly, they're going to say, "Come on over," but who are they letting into their house? They don't know. It's crazy. I would never have thought about it, I'll be honest with you, even if I wasn't an agent.

If you were to get a call from a family member in another state wanting to sell their home, what advice would you give them about selecting an agent who can best serve their needs?

I would tell them that I would find them an agent up there to help them out, that I would do the screening process for them. We have 120,000 agents nationwide right now, so I'm sure that we could find someone that would help them sell their home, get it sold as quickly as possible and get things done. It's definitely a huge referral network. We work in a family, so we call it KW Agent-to-KW Agent and find someone to get it done. We're pretty well trained, for the most part, in the business, better than anyone else as far as I'm concerned.

We can definitely do help someone find an agent in another part of the country, and then when they get down here, we'll take a run with it. We know the area better than anyone else. I've lived here all my life, so

I definitely know just about all the areas that they may appeal to their needs.

I think you have to find out your seller's profile, you know what I'm saying? Because people are different and you have to know their personality, what they do for a living, and what's important to them when you first do the screening process for the seller. You find out what's important to them, how they liked their last agent, what they did not like about the last agent, how they want to communicate, what they think needs to be done, and all that stuff because a lot of times what they think needs to be done is totally opposite of what you think they need to do. Either that or they did it or they said they did it, but they have to do it again.

You just touch on the situation and find out who's happy about the relocation. Is the buyer happy? The seller? Is it the husband or the wife or the kids? Who's not happy? You find that out and you let that agent know, going in there, this is what you're walking into. I think a lot of times agents just do a referral and don't do any kind of background check or give the referral a scoop of what's going on there. We'll walk right in to be side-blinded and it's not fun to have it known that you walked in unprepared. But if you go in there prepared, knowing that the wife is happy about going, the husband's not happy about going, the kids are unhappy about going, and these are their concerns about moving, these are their concerns about losing their house, things will go more smoothly.

I think it's just a matter of sitting down with the seller and finding out what their needs are. You sit down and talk and then you call the broker in their area and you tell them, "This is what I have and this is the situation. Who is your best agent, one that is going to take care of this client for me?" It's best to go that route.

How can someone who needs a real estate agent find out more about you and how you can help?

They can contact us at 678-631-1788 or they can contact me via email at jerome@jeromejsmith.com.

Top Agent Barry Burnett

Barry Burnett is CEO of Barry Burnett Realty, based out of Burbank, California. Since 1973, Barry Burnett has served as a leading real estate advisor, helping clients across the U.S. and internationally to build wealth and the life and legacy they desire.

Barry has been a full-service realtor for 43 years. He's personally closed over 4,000 real estate transactions for his clients and partners. He's conducted business in numerous states, he's done residential sales and development all the way to industrial and commercial sales and development, re-having, re-positioning, investor coordination, and all points in between.

He's also taught real estate at universities in several states and he's served as an expert witness in the federal Los Angeles and Southern California court systems. He has also managed major transactions for extremely wealthy clients, as well as helping beginner investors build their holdings step-by-step and helping protect them.

What led you into real estate? Was it something you always knew you wanted to do or did you stumble into it?

It was a complete and total right turn from the path that I had anticipated. I was a student at UCLA, a Chemistry major pretty much guaranteed to be going to UCLA Medical School. At 19, as a second-semester junior, I realized that I really wanted to get married and I didn't want my wife to have to support me through medical school.

I started looking at the options and I'd been getting unsolicited offers to do stuff from the time I was about 16. They were all highly high paid jobs, but didn't require a doctorate, let alone a masters, or even college degree. I thought, "Wow, let me look at what the options are." I realized that in real estate, an individual who is prepared in his heart to be a servant, can start off with very little investment and control a tremendous amount of inventory and opportunity for people or for institutions or for whatever.

I personally have never chosen to serve institutional investors or institutions; I really want to deal with individuals. That's how I realized it, If I've got an unlimited opportunity, I'm going into real estate. At 19, I started.

What personal attributes, traits, or qualities do you think have most contributed to your success and how do you think you've developed these?

That's an all-encompassing question. I'm an individual of great faith in a loving God who has commissioned me to represent him and in doing that I have to focus on what's really important. What's really important is to love one another and treat others as more important than myself. To the extent that I do that, I'm a better servant; to the extent that I don't, I just sort of mess up and flounder.

I discovered almost immediately that to the extent that it's about me, my enthusiasm is going to get people interested, but it's not necessarily right for them. In my first year, I lost half of the money I put into escrow because I had "sold" as opposed to counseled or assisted and coordinated.

When my enthusiasm and my vision for someone else's benefit and welfare wasn't what was right for them, the transactions rightfully unraveled. I'd still closed a tremendous amount of business, but I did it wrong. Everything changed after I did my analysis of my first year's production and I realized, "Oh, it has nothing to do with me. If I'm serving correctly, then I'm gonna be listening a great deal more and finding out how to meet people's needs."

I believe that it's important to serve, but to serve as a surrogate sometimes you have to draw people forward or lead them into hearing

49

what they're saying. Sometimes you repeat back what somebody tells you and ask them if they agree with it and if it's what they really meant. This is important because it may be totally different from the way they were seeing it in their mind's eye.

To be a servant, you have to kind of look around the edges and look around the corners. In my career, I've had the privilege of training somewhere between 1,200 and 1,500 agents. There's only one message that I can effectively teach and it's extremely, extremely brief. All of the training comes down to this one thing, "Find a need, fill the need."

I'm less interested in what somebody's wants; I'm extremely interested in their legitimate needs. If their legitimate need matches my ability to coordinate and assist effectively and efficiently, then I want to fill their need and I've been fairly successful at it.

What were some of the major adversities and trials you had to overcome to achieve your goals?

I wish you could have just heard me laughing at myself. I've had a blast in my years and I have done a lot of extraordinary things. There are others in our field that absolutely daunt me when I look at their triumphs and successes and the number of things they accomplish. I've been rich and I've been broke six times and I've never been poor. To me poor says, "I don't really think I can do it, so I'm not gonna try."

Rich and poor are opposite sides of the same coin. My efforts may reward me at times, if I'm focused and if I'm being a good servant. On the other hand, I've been embezzled a number of times for multi-million dollars and it's pretty awkward. You can't stop trusting in people, but I have shifted and now the only one that I will partner with, where I'm not the sole managing partner, is my wife, and she's the boss anyway.

What kept you going despite these obstacles? Why didn't you give up?

I'll give you two examples. One, the evening before my 30th birthday, one of my partners called to wish me a happy birthday and "Oh, by the way, you're out of the company." I was stunned, "Out of the company? How, how can you do that? I'm a full partner and there are three of us. We built this partnership corporation into a really strong team." He said, "Well no, I'm just gonna tell you, you're out." He said, "I've moved all of the assets to a subordinate company, I've bankrupted the parent company, I've bankrupted the second company, I've moved all the assets three corporations deep. There is no bankruptcy court in the land that could possibly re-amass the real estate and the holdings before I can get rid of it, so you're just out." "Okay."

That was $11 million. The next morning I had $4,300 to start life over again. I was married with 7-year-old twins and the next morning we looked at each other and we said, "Okay, let's start over," and we did.

Four weeks later I had 27 houses coming out of the ground and was in the process of selling them, so that we could get housing for people.

When my partner took my money, he didn't take my heart, he didn't take my right to serve, he didn't take my contacts, he didn't take my emotions – he just stole money. That's horrible of him, but if I gave myself away for that cheap, well that would have been a shame. I started again.

I've never met a man or a woman who hasn't faced extraordinary adversity. I applaud the ones that face it with courage and I applaud the ones that repent of their fears. Because while we have breathe and life, we have the opportunity to progress, we have the right to choose. In fact, it's more than a right to choose; we have the responsibility to choose.

I mentioned there were two. The second example I think is probably a little bit more of where I live. Twelve years ago I had a motorcycle accident. I was out looking at real estate and sometimes the best way to see real estate is without looking through a rooftop or a car door or car window. I was out looking at real estate in Pasadena, California on my motorcycle and right below the Rose Bowl there is a magnificent, very enigmatic bridge that has spectacular arches right where the Rose Parade begins.

I was going to cross that bridge at sunset because I'm a romantic at heart and I just wanted to see that bridge at sunset. I get out towards the bridge and somebody's transmission fluid had leaked. The transmission had erupted right there in the middle of a small turn. I hit the transmission fluid at 30 miles an hour, went into the guard rail, and left my right leg 250 yards behind me. I actually had time to say two things out loud. One was, "Lord, okay, see you in a second," and the next one coming off of the guard rail was, "Well, that ain't gonna grow back."

I was still up and at that point to get run over on the motor cycle would have just been rude. I pulled into the middle of the bridge, set the bike down, pulled out my cell phone, dialed 911 and put it aside, grabbed my belt, and set my tourniquet. I was very fortunate. I was enormously fortunate that the Lord gave me the tenacity to stay with it and keep the tourniquet held.

Well, it's been 12 years and in the hospital operating theater, when they were cleaning up from the accident, it's hard to keep an operating theater clean, what happened to me was I got the MRSA, the flesh-eating disease, but it didn't go into my tissue; it went to my bone marrow.

Over the next two years the bone kept dying off and they had to keep cutting. It went from the middle of my shin to where it is now, about four and a half inches above my knee joint. I can guarantee you this. You don't want to get into a foot race with a one-legged realtor because I'll win every time.

Let me give you some insight into the realities of being a boy scout. Boy Scouts of America trained me from the age of 8 to the age of

18 to be prepared. 'BE PREPARED' is their motto and I was. I had been the kid that you could put out in a desert with a fork and a wax-covered kitchen match and say, "Here, be here at 1700 Sunday," and I'd go off with a smile. I was prepared for the trouble.

Everybody needs to be prepared because life has troubles. It comes in different shapes and sizes, but again, you have to make the choice. If I had chosen to say, "Oh well, it's me, I'm in terrible shape," then yes, I absolutely would have died. There's not a possibility I could have lived through that, but I made choices and everybody has to make those choices at some point. It may be any level of catastrophe in their lives, but they can still make the choice to carry on.

What do you see in your vision for the way your business is going to grow, say over the next 5 years?

It goes back to "find a need, fill the need." I wake up every day, as if I'm unemployed, until I find somebody's need or address somebody's need that I'm already aware of. When I do that, I don't have to worry about whether my plate's full or empty, it's always full. I'm always looking to solve something that someone's laid in front of me.

In the real estate business, people have to prospect. I don't prospect; I look for needs and I don't care where I find them. If they're authentic and if I can coordinate with that particular individual or a family, then I'm the guy. Over the next five years, that's what I plan to do. In fact, I'm 43 years into it. I only have 17 more years to get my 60-

year pin, then I'm out of here. Then you'll have to deal with my grandkids.

What do you feel is the best way you market yourself as a real estate professional for continual growth?

You can't find people's needs unless you work where people are and no one's going to volunteer their needs unless you're asking authentic questions. If you're just giving them the perfunctory, "Hey, how you doin'?" then they're going to shake your hand and that's that, but if the questions are authentic and if the care and concern is legitimate, then people will open up about what they need and you can decide whether you're the right person to help them.

We all have stuff to do and I've got responsibilities. If I accept somebody's need as something I can fulfill, then I have a responsibility. You can't be a secret agent. You have to be where people are and you have to be asking questions. It doesn't matter where it is, whether you're in the lunch line or calling Uber or standing at the airport.

What's the biggest misconception/myth that people have about working with a real estate agent?

People are people. If they have trust, if the trust is earned, then there are very few misconceptions. Unfortunately, many times there isn't that sense of trust. When that occurs, the misconception is that the real estate agent is trying to be self-serving or is looking after the almighty dollar. Unfortunately, people are people and some of them are self-serving and that limits their ability to serve others. If someone finds that kind of agent, they should be looking for a totally different mindset and totally different agent.

When you walk into an open house for example, you're out kicking tires and you're looking around in Florida and you are wandering around to look at the property. You want to know that the agent is going to allow you to see what you see and then ask and respond to authentic questions that have to do with you, not to do with the agent. If you find that, then the buyers of any property have to realize that they don't have to stand on tradition,; and according to the National Realtors Code of Ethics, the buyer has the right to select their representative. They should have that right and they should choose very carefully.

The misconception is that sometimes you walk into an open house and you feel stuck, that you have to use somebody in whom you may not have trust or confidence. That's a misconception. You have the right to choose and you should.

If you were to get a call from a family member in another state wanting to sell their home, what advice would you give them about selecting an agent who can best serve their needs?

Relationship is extremely important. The relationship between the buyer, my family member or my referral, who I treat just as if they were family members, has to be greeted in the same way that I would

56

greet that business, that I have a responsibility. They have to find somebody who accepts the responsibility of serving them.

Now, it doesn't mean that clients can be irresponsible about your demands for service. Some people call at 10 O'clock at night. That's unreasonable. That's unrealistic and it's inappropriate. Some people expect that an agent is going to live 24/7 in the real estate business, and if I call, they need to answer. That's also inappropriate and it's unrealistic and demeaning. You need to find somebody who shares a commonality of values.

With the internet, you can find a whole lot about people, even brand spanking new agents. You can find out what they've done in the past and whether they've been serving target or they've just been money beasts. You can find out a lot about people before you ever spend much time with them, face-to-face, but a conversation needs to happen. You have to have a commonality, a sense of mutual respect, and if there is a mutual respect, then the job can be done. If you're communicating honestly about your needs, then they can fulfill those needs honestly.

If you're looking at somebody who tells you their need and you are listening, you sometimes have to tell them, "Okay, this particular property, it may not actually serve your need because of this and this and this, but let's look at the broader perspective. This is what you said is your need; let's look to fulfill that." Then it's less of a property question and more of a needs-fulfillment question. Would you agree?

How can someone that needs a real estate agent find out more about you and how you can help?

I'm delighted that you asked that question, but I'm just a little guy. What everybody needs to do is a Personal Needs Assessment and find somebody in their bailiwick, in their heart of hearts that can fulfill their needs. If they want to reach me, I'm at www.barryburnett.net.

That's my website and it's an easy one, but there are an awful lot of folks around the country with far greater skills and far greater desires and endeavors and probably a whole lot closer to them. It doesn't mean I can't serve them in multiple states or around the world. I've got a magnificent 9,500-square-foot villa that I'm going to be putting on the market next week just south of Milano in Italy, in the town Lodi.

If you have a desire for that, then come on, it's spectacular, but as far as what your needs are, there are a lot of people who can fulfill them. You just have to be responsible to yourself and take the time to find the people who are interested in your needs above their own.

Top Agent Shirley Weems

Shirley Weems is with Waterman Real Estate out of Brevard County, Florida. Shirley ranks as one of the nation's Top 250 Realtors in the country by Real Trends for 2013, 2014, and 2015. She has sold over 1,000 units since 2007. She's also received the Quality Service Award from 2007 to 2013, the Centurion Award for Volume in Sales from 2010 to 2013, and top producer awards since 2007.

She's residential, relocation, short sale, and REO certified. When she's not working real estate, she is also featured on the AM radio Financial News talk show with Michael Terrio of the Terrio Group and she has been featured as a panel member for the Women's Real Estate Conference.

What led you to real estate? Was it something you always knew you wanted to do?

Actually, I definitely stumbled into it. I was previously a nine-to-five employee. Actually, I was in law enforcement with the state of Florida. That definitely takes its toll on you. You work long hours in the most depressing situations. I actually took the opportunity when I had maternity leave to look into getting into something else. Real estate, believe it or not, is pretty easy to get into as far as licensing goes, and testing, and schooling, so that's how I fell into it.

What personal attributes, traits, or qualities have most contributed to your success and how did you develop these?

My parents are from a family of workaholics. For my parents, and their parents before them, stopping wasn't even an option. That, along with my own hyper-ness, I guess that's the best way to put it, is a very good match. It's never enough for me. I don't know when to quit and that's what I was always noticing in real life. When you're on the same level as the folks beside you, everybody's making the same amount of money, everybody's getting the same amount of work to do, those who are better, faster, and more efficient just get more work. The pay doesn't go up. The time you spend at work doesn't go down. You just get more to fill your time and you end up doing more work than the person beside you making the same amount of money and not really benefiting from your efficiency and your productivity. I think that a commission-based job was right up my alley, based on family, background, and my own personality traits.

What were some of the major adversities and trials you had to overcome to achieve your goals?

Heartbreak is for sure something that you have to be able to deal with, being able to juggle your family is just huge, huge. A lot of people that get into real estate don't realize that if your spouse doesn't support you, if your children don't support you, if the people around you don't support you, then this is not going to help you be successful by any means. Learning to deal with spending time with people who are not committed to you is important. Months and months of phone calls, conversations, et cetera, et cetera, and it leads to nothing. They end up possibly not pursuing that avenue, possibly using another real estate agent. It's something that you have to learn to deal with very, very quickly, or it's going to take a huge toll. Fortunately for me, my husband is an amazing person, who can deal with the fact that, "Okay, I can't be there. I'm running late. Can you go get the kids? I can't make it. Can you do this? Can you do this?" It was just fantastic that I was able to have that. I would've never been able to do it otherwise.

What kept you going despite these obstacles? Why didn't you give up?

This is a job where you can make as much or as little as you want. The truth is, there is nothing else I can even dream of getting into with the ability to make this much money. In the end, unfortunately, I'm not doing what I love and what I wish to do, which actually goes back to law enforcement. If the FBI called me right now and said, "We want you, but we're not paying you at all." I would say, "No problem. I'll be there." I would do it for free. That is what I love. I love the courtrooms and I love the legal world in general, all of it. My degree's actually in psychology.

Initially, that was my goal, but let's face it, the easiest way to get to the end of the rainbow is acquiring the money that you need to get there and real estate offers that if you're not afraid to work and go get it. At this point, to walk away would be like walking away from a lottery ticket that I have figured out. It wouldn't make much sense. That definitely keeps me going, the ability to keep making money, be smart enough to do the right things with it, put it away, and hopefully not have to wait until I'm 75 or 65 to retire.

What is your vision for your career for the next five years?

Honestly, my plan is to hopefully retire. I have been really, really fortunate in what seems to have been a bad time to start was actually a blessing. Because I started when I did, I was smart enough to go where the market was going, which led me into the foreclosure and the short sales, which then led me into meeting some very powerful, wise investors who have been doing this for thirty years, and their fathers were doing it for thirty years before them. There's a very, very small handful of people who are true investors and I got very, very lucky to meet three or four of them who actually took me under their wing and taught me more about real estate than just being a realtor.

They taught me the investment side of it, being able to allocate money, knowing how to deal with rentals, and funding, and hard money, and financing, just all these things that I've been able to learn and use. Right now, I'm hoping to actually scale back in the next five years from the general real estate side and go into more of the investing side. I do run my own office. We have roughly fourteen agents in my branch. I really like training and I really like watching other people that I trained grow. I would really like to focus more on training them and letting them do the hard work so I can actually go home at 5:00 and not work twenty-four hours a day anymore. That's my hope.

What do you feel is the best way you market yourself as a real estate professional for continual growth?

Right now, when it comes to the area in which I live, marketing is fortunately not something that I have to spend a lot of money or a lot of time on. I don't have huge competition. There are a great deal of realtors in the area, but only a handful in our entire county that are full-time for high-producing volume agents. I've become pretty well-known, which is nice because my referral business and the folks that know me know how I operate and how we get the job done. I think, right now, all the signs around town that I have is really my number one marketing skill, being able to just continue to get listings, to be able to continue to put those signs up in people's yards.

In the end, I'm here for everybody. I even have agents from other companies who call me instead of their own brokers to get advice. I love that. Nothing makes me happier than that. No amount of money in the world says more than somebody just calling me from a totally different company and asking me because they know that I can help them. That's really, I think, all the marketing I need at this point and I'm going to keep flourishing on that and keep being there for people who call me, as well as my clients and colleagues.

What's the biggest misconception/myth that people have about working with a real estate agent?

From the public's point of view, they think we're all the same. That is, one of my biggest frustrations about real estate. This is the one position that I've ever had where my resume really doesn't impress anybody. I have rarely gotten a phone call from a person who did not know me, a client who did not know me in some shape or form, who said to me, "I looked up your resume and it is impressive. I want the best to be on my team and work for me." Real estate is the one profession that seems to go a lot more on "who do you know," and that is frustration to me because I do well.

I want to be rewarded for doing well, not just with money and with a prize, but with people actually seeing that and seeing that there's a difference. When you try to find an attorney, you look to see who the best one is, who's won the most cases. When you get ready to go a surgeon, you want to go to the one who's done the most surgeries, who's familiar with your specific ailment. In real estate, it doesn't seem to matter. If you have a real estate license and you're a friend of a friend of a friend who might not have sold a home within the last twelve months, it makes no difference to the public. They're going to use that friend because it's a friend of a friend of a friend.

That is something that I wish the public really understood and that they knew the difference between us. There's a reason that there is a difference between us. We have 3,300 agents in our county and the same 40 or 50 do well. That's a really small percentage. Out of 3,300 agents, 1,700 of them did not even sell one home last year. The public doesn't know this. They just think that we're all the same. I wish there was a way to get that message across. It's no different than getting in a plane with a pilot who hasn't flown in two years. I'm not getting on that plane.

If you were to get a call from a family member in another state wanting to sell their home, what advice would you give them about selecting an agent who can best serve their needs?

Okay, here's the funny thing. If you are a buyer looking for an agent, I would tell you to go find someone who is fairly new, but with a trainer or with a broker who has a strong resume. The reason I say fairly new on the buyer side is because buyers need a lot of attention. They want to see properties. They have a lot of questions. They will call and you need to be there to answer the phone. Somebody who is too busy or who is primarily a listing agent sometimes will have a hard time giving that person enough attention to make them feel warm and fuzzy.

The truth is they don't need that much attention, but they think they need that much attention. If you don't provide it to them, they will spend time with you, but then they will end up using someone else anyway because they feel neglected. With that being said, that new agent doesn't know a lot about the financing and the inspections and appraisals and surveys and all the other fun things that come with buying a home, which is why I say they need to have a very strong trainer, manager, or broker who themselves have been in the business and sold in the business. Not someone who just held a license for the last twenty years, but actually sells and actually operates and functions and does transactions.

On the seller's side, though, it's the opposite. If you're looking for an agent to sell your home, you need a listing agent who already has a lot of listings. The agent who has a lot of listings has a lot of people in the office to take the calls that come in on the home, a lot of agents in the office ready to jump up and show that property, a lot of strong backing, the money to market, the connections to market. If somebody only has had one listing, four listings, five, ten listings, chances are that person's not making a whole lot and doesn't have the connections that somebody with a lot of listings would have, which means they probably don't have the knowledge and the funds, as well as other agents in the office, to help sell your property. Does that make sense?

Believe it or not, in school they do not really teach you anything you need to know when you actually come out into the real world of real estate. VA financing and FHA financing, for instance, have requirements and regulations. A house has to be in a certain condition. New agents tend to not know these things, tend to take clients to houses that would never qualify for this type of financing, yet they're taking you there because they don't know any better. It's just things like that that you really need to learn once you get out here. It's not something that you're taught in school. That trainer, office trainer, office manager, needs to go over, "What do you have? What is your client looking for? What are they financed with?" Then, give them a run-down of how to proceed.

If somebody wants to learn more about you and what you have to offer, what's the best place for people to go?

I would tell you to me Facebook is probably, honestly, the best place. Find my Facebook page by looking up Weem's Team Brevard and the phone number attached to that is 321-900-9900. Because of my name, I'm a rare internet Google search, so just searching my name. You will definitely find me everywhere. We have websites and things of that nature, but I much rather people call me if they get into buying or selling mode, so we can really discuss their situation one-on-one. Everybody's situation's different. I don't really like sending people to websites for information because it might not pertain to them and all it does is confuse them further.

Top Agent Addora Beall

Addora Beall is a Broker Associate with Hall and Chambers Real Estate out of California. Addora is a hyper local real estate professional focusing her energies on residential real estate with an emphasis on architecturally significant homes in premier areas of Glendale, California and surrounding areas.

She's a licensed Broker and has been in business for 17 years. She was recognized in 2013 and 2014 as one of Southern California's Top 50 Agents. She is the President Elect for Glendale Association of REALTORS®.

What led you to real estate? Was it something you always knew you wanted to do?

That's an interesting question. I never thought of it until my husband suggested it. I had been an interior designer and I was getting a little bit weary of that business. He said, "You know what? Why don't you try real estate? I think you'd be really good." I passed the test and started selling real estate. It was just a natural evolution for me. I never had a learning curve. It was always comfortable for me.

I think it's great that when you chose a path that you didn't expect, that you just fell into it naturally, like you said, it's almost like it was your calling to be in it because it was so easy for you.

What personal attributes, traits, or qualities have contributed the most to your success and how did you develop these?

I'm not afraid to tell clients the truth. I think many times agents in interviews with their potential clients will tell them what they want to hear and I'm not that person. I do believe that prospective clients and clients who actually end up working with me will agree with that. They want to know the truth. People who are sufficiently motivated to list or sell a home want the truth. People have told me they find it refreshing.

They don't want to mess around with me telling them an inflated price and having it sit on the market for a long time. They want me to get the job done and I am able to do that. I'm also not afraid to ask pertinent questions. In the past, I've done some training and mentoring of new agents. I've found that they're afraid to ask the questions that are so relevant to their business. I'm not afraid to do that.

I think you have to really drill down to the motivation of why a potential client wants to sell or buy a home. Unless you are really in touch with that point, you're not going to be successful in a transaction. Does that make sense?

I have a heart to serve rather than to sell. In that, I take away the big piece of my potential commission because that's just a benefit of a job well done, in my opinion. If I really am listening and caring and putting a potential client's interest in front of my own, I'm going to do an excellent job for them and everyone is going to be happy in the end.

To be honest, I have made choices in some interviews not to accept a listing or to work with a buyer because it wasn't a good fit for either of us. I think that's really important. You have to be comfortable with each other. We have to forge a bond of trust in order to do a good job.

Can you give specific examples of when these traits have played a role in your path toward success?

I deal with a lot of families who are out of the area who have a parent who has died or they are relocating them to assisted living. Oftentimes, these are painful situations. Maybe a family member has just passed away or they have had to relocate them to senior living or whatever. My sensitivity and desire to serve them has been at the forefront. It has created a sense of comfort in a difficult situation. I think it has served me well.

What were some of the major adversities and trials that you had to overcome to achieve your goals?

The market decline from 2009 to 2012 just about laid me bare. It caused me to rethink how I did business and what I was going to do to continue. I changed companies and I got involved in personal coaching, which gave me an all new skill set to be more successful. I think that was my saving grace. It took me to the next level in my real estate career and I've never looked back.

The market from 2009 to 2012 was the time where we had lots and lots of short sales and bank-owned properties, which is a segment of the market in which I had never participated. I jumped into that full blown and started working at a company that only worked on that kind of property. It allowed me to make it through that difficult few years when regular retail real estate was virtually nonexistent.

What kept you going despite these obstacles? Why didn't you give up?

I love the business of real estate. As I said, there was no learning curve for me. It just felt natural to me. Self-preservation is what caused me to move forward. I had a family to support and I would not, could not let them down. I had to recreate myself and my business and make the most of it and that is what I did.

I think it's very important to understand my motivation. Anyone in this business has to know why they do what they do or they will quickly become a statistic. One must understand their "why."

What is your vision for your career for the next five years?

I've thought about this for a number or years. I think the time is coming to fruition for me to think about building a dynamic team. I have a passion for training new agents. I want to incorporate them into my business model. I want to expand what I do and do it better. I think bringing in some agents, starting with buyer's agents and maybe another listing agent down the road. I'm not sure yet. I'm still formulating that. I think that's the next step for me.

What do you feel is the best way you market yourself as a real estate professional for continual growth?

I think it's important to understand yourself and to know what you're really good at. For example, this little niche market with trust work that has been created for me in recent years. I have a lot of compassion for families that are going through difficult times and it has kind of evolved. It seems to be a very good fit for me, whereas some people might really want to work with really high-dollar properties and be all about the money. I think you have to figure out what you're good at and then find a way in the market to manifest that.

It doesn't feel like work. I work really hard. I work probably some every day. I don't take a lot of time off because I love it. I love doing what I do and I think my clients recognize that and appreciate it.

What's the biggest misconception/myth that people have about working with a real estate agent?

I think it's that all agents are alike. I think once you get into working with a really excellent agent, you understand the difference because there is a huge difference. In a good market, like we're in now, a seller's market, it seems that new agents pop up all over the place because they want to "get rich quick." I think their business acumen reflects that. They don't really serve their clients.

They just want to get them sold. They just want to get to the commission the quickest easiest way they can and they cut corners. I think it gives a good ethical agent with integrity a bad rap because the perception is that all agents are alike and all agents just want that commission. I think that's so untrue and unfair. Once you work with a really excellent agent, you understand that.

If you were to get a call from a family member in another state wanting to sell their home, what advice would you give them about selecting an agent who can best serve their needs?

I would look for a seasoned agent who has some type of a paper trail on the internet. See who they are and what they do. Perhaps a Zillow or something like that where you have client comments. I would look for an agent that does a lot of business in the area that the client wants to work in.

I would see if they've been in business at least ten years and look for their areas of specialty. Maybe they might specialize in relocation or something like that. Then I would read the reviews from past clients.

Everybody uses the internet for research and reviews. By the time they get to the point of calling an agent for an interview, they already know everything about them. It's quite interesting. I find it all the time. I ask people who call me to see if we can get together and talk about listing a home, I ask them every time, "Where did you find me?" "I found you on the internet." Well, great. They've gone to my Zillow page and looked at my client reviews. It feels like a good fit for them and they call me. They find me in other places as well, such as my web-site and my top agent magazine, a number of places.

How can someone that needs a real estate agent find out more about you and how you can help?

They can go to LivinginGlendale.com, which is my web-site, or they could go to Zillow.com and type in my name, Addora Beall, and read my client endorsements, or they can just put my name on Google and see what comes up. There's a wealth of information and my contact information is there.

Top Agent Shayla Twit

Shayla Twit is a luxury realtor with RE/MAX Alliance Group, based out of Sarasota, Florida. Shayla carries a long list of accommodations, including more five-star reviews than anyone else in her market. She has achieved the RE/MAX 100% Club, Gold Club, and Platinum Club Awards, ranking her in the top 1% at both her local Board of Realtors, as well as statewide.

She's also been featured in 'Top Agent Magazine' for Florida and she's been seen on Home Castle TV channel 7's 'Out and About Southwest Florida,' and just recently she shot an episode on HDTV's 'Beachfront Bargain Hunt' on Siesta Key. She specializes in both luxury and waterfront properties. On top of all that, she found time to not only speak to people in English, but she also speaks French and Turkish.

What led you to real estate? Was it something you always knew you wanted to do?

It's not something I always dreamt of doing. I moved to Sarasota and everywhere we went people were talking about real estate. The more I thought about it, the more I thought I want to be my own boss. I want to be able to have unlimited income, flexible hours, have my own schedule, and all of those components. I just felt that I would enjoy it, which I think is really important, and do well at it. I really love the business and it's been 15+ years strong, so that's pretty much how I landed into it. There have been a lot of ups and downs, but I'm glad I ended up in this business.

What personal attributes, traits, or qualities have most contributed to your success and how did you develop these?

I grew up in the Midwest and I was always taught from a very young age to work for what you want, go after it. Nobody is going to give you anything in life. For me it's waking up early, getting after it every day, and never giving up. You have to reach for it because people aren't going to come to you. You have to find a way for people to find you and want to work with you.

Just the sheer dedication that this business takes, it's not for everybody. You basically wake up without the guarantee of a paycheck, but guaranteed expenses. You really do have to be very motivated, very organized. I think that those are some of the attributes that I really have honed in on and at which I have really become an expert.

Can you give specific examples of when these traits have played a role in your path toward success?

There have been a lot of ups and downs. When I started in this business, it was very easy because the market was really good. When the market is good, it tends to be a little bit easier for people to make a sale, but the market crashed and then it's like, "Okay, who's going to survive this?" Especially when I was newer and young, right out of college, I tried to break into that luxury market from the get-go. And it was a struggle.

I actually had an opportunity to speak with someone who owns a boutique on one of the islands. He was a referral from someone in my network. He spoke down to me, stating something to the effect, "You know what? It's going to take a long time for you to break into this market. These people have been around a long time. You can't just walk in here and sell these people." It was such vivid conversation that I recall it 15 years later and it drives me. It drives me to succeed, wake up every morning and prove that person wrong, not just for him, but for myself. That was kind of a breaking moment for me in the business.

What were some of the major adversities and trials you had to overcome to achieve your goals?

When the market crashed, that was a turning point for me. It was at that time that I was carrying a few different properties, and like a lot of people, I ended up losing everything because not only was my income dependent on selling, but I had these properties to maintain and it just got to be too much. I had to swallow some pride and kind of set the refresh button and start over again.

Thankfully, I started over in my 20s, so I was able to bounce back. It was a huge learning lesson. After that, I became really very conservative and more fine-tuned than ever in terms of marketing strategies, what I needed to spend, how I was going to conduct myself, and how I was going to get into that next level. That was the biggest turning point of my entire career. It was nice to have the ability to restart and really have a fresh stab at the business. I guess it was a blessing in disguise, but it was a challenge, no doubt.

What kept you going despite these obstacles? Why didn't you give up?

The only other option for me in my mind, had real estate not worked out, was to go to law school, instead. It was the only other avenue that I figured I would enjoy and do well at. So, instead I stayed the course, feeling like I could make a breakthrough in real estate. The passion was there. I wanted to assist people in realizing their real estate dreams. It was a long road after that, but eventually I did break through.

Actually, I had family members who always supported me, even though they questioned me a couple of times, "Are you sure you're in the right business?" I actually never wavered once. I never questioned whether this was what I wanted to do for my career. Thankfully, the last several years have been very good to me and I've proven to myself that it can work.

I look at some of these Realtors out there who've sold multi-millions each year and I figure if this person can do it, I sure as heck can. That's been a cool component as far as having mentors in the business to look up to and say, "Okay, this guy is doing this and this person." I feel like I can get to that level too. You have all these people who have been in the business maybe twice as long as me.

I'm thinking I'm rubbing elbows with them now. We're doing deals together. It's a really good feeling to have that, finally getting to that point where I've always wanted to be. There's always room for growth. There's always room for learning. I'm learning every day, with every transaction. I'm learning from my peers and everyone around me. Every day is a new development, it seems.

What is your vision for your career for the next five years?

That's a good question. I think that ideally I'd like to be just selling on the islands. I love island living, that lifestyle and the water! It helps me help the client even more because I know that area inside and out. I think when you're a little scattered in terms of area, it doesn't help the client as much, but that would be my goal to focus most of my business out there. I receive a lot of repeat and referral clients who ask about all areas of Sarasota, so I'm sure to either assist them myself or at a minimum have someone on my team work directly with them. And I'll continue doing so.

It's always a compliment to get referrals, but outside of that, I think having a full-time assistant would be another goal. I currently have a part-time helper that assists me with runaround errands and doing other time-consuming tasks, but having someone full-time would help me do what I love even more. Long term, though, I prefer to keep my team small, not to grow too big too fast because I want to maintain quality at all times.

I currently have two buyers' agents to whom I consistently disperse leads. I don't believe that bigger is always better. In addition, I'd like to fine tune more of my marketing strategies, perhaps expand that a little bit, and like I said, maybe get a little bit more consistent help with some type of an assistant.

What do you feel is the best way you market yourself as a real estate professional for continual growth?

I do spend a significant amount advertising online. But really I do get a lot of repeat and referral clients. Because I've been selling so long, the phone rings! I receive referrals from the RE/MAX network nationwide. This has been an excellent resource not only for me, but for the exposure it brings to my clients.

Everybody knows the name and a lot of agents from out of the state or out of the area who don't even know me, they reach out to me and we've got that going for us. That's been wonderful. Like I said, my clients are the best source of referrals. They know because they've worked with me. They were happy, obviously. They're referring. I've always been of the mindset that I'd rather keep the client and lose the deal because it's just a deal.

If it's not in their best interest and they're not happy, they're going to tell people that they're not happy. I'd rather keep them happy, do the right thing always, and it will always come back to you tenfold. That has been my experience.

What's the biggest misconception/myth that people have about working with a real estate agent?

One thing that stands out is that folks think that Realtors make so much money, but people don't see the backend of things, the ad dollars, the hours we spend, the failures we must overcome, the deals that have died that we have to resuscitate, so to speak. There's just a lot that goes into it behind the scenes. Then they say your checks are huge, but you only spent so much time, but there's so much more that goes into it that justifies those checks.

Not only that, but there are part-time Realtors, which is fine, but I am a full-time professional real estate agent, and if you text me or you e-mail me, I'm very quick to respond. There's no delay. I'm on top of the file before things can even go wrong. I'm done before the other parties to the contract can even ask me to do the next item on the check list. There's a lot to be said for that. Saving time and being efficient.

The other thing I think is just that it's easy to make a sale. There are so many intricate details to a contract, legalities, making sure that you're looking out for your client and keeping in contract with them, making sure that they're not in default or losing their escrow deposits, making sure to have good contacts in the business. Like I said, I've been doing this for 15 years. There are plenty of agents who've done it a lot longer.

I've fine-tuned my vendor list, such as inspectors, lenders, appraisers, attorneys, contractors, etc., all those components that come together and really assist the client. That's the bottom line, helping the client.

If you were to get a call from a family member in another state wanting to sell their home, what advice would you give them about selecting an agent who can best serve their needs?

I'd probably want to help them with it, but if they wanted to do it on their own, I would tell them to start with the RE/MAX network because I'm obviously partial to RE/MAX. And they're everywhere. Chances are good there is a RE/MAX agent close by. Look at their page. Look at how detailed it is. See what they've sold and compare it to what you're selling.

Ask yourself if that person would be familiar with that neighborhood's prices, etc., and whether they would be a good fit in terms of how they appear to do business. Also, I recommend cross referencing it with their reviews. These reviews are scrubbed by the Zillow/Trulia systems so you know that they're valid. So it's helpful to get a third party's opinion. Agents pay for this system and are either active with it or not. So it shows that they're going that "extra mile."

I can't tell you how many clients have called me and said, "Hey, we've read through your reviews. We don't know you, but it seems like you would be a good fit." That is how they start the conversation. And of course I'd be happy to do some more digging for them, but I think that's a great place to start for anybody.

Obviously, a referral from somebody that you know is also an option, but being able to see that an agent is very active online and being able to do a little bit of background checking is important. I have a lot of clients that do this. Well, maybe not a full background check, but they do a lot of digging around online to find out about me. And I'm everywhere. If you Google my name, you can see a lot of information about me in the business world and see where I'm from and what I've done and all that kind of stuff. It's helpful for someone who doesn't know you.

How can someone who needs a real estate agent find out more about you and how you can help?

I'm at www.SarasotaRealProperty.com. From there, you can find my cell and my e-mail and some of the blogs I've done. All that good stuff.

Top Agent Kathleen Monroe

Kathleen Monroe is with Evergreen Realty out of Irvine, California. Inspired by her father's success, Kathleen followed in her father's footsteps as a top-producing real estate professional, starting out as Rookie of the Year, she went on to garner accolades consistently in Orange Coast Magazine as a 5-star realtor. Less than 3% of the realtors in Orange County receive this distinguished honor. Kathleen has also been featured on the cover of Top Agent Magazine in 2014 and 2015.

Per Kathleen's client, Nancy Brodsky, *"Kathleen has an upbeat personality, great sense of humor, and uncompromising knowledge of the real estate market."*

What led you to real estate? Was it something you always knew you wanted to do?

Well, for many years I wanted to be a realtor. Of course, growing up with my father, who had the most amazing work ethic, and witnessing firsthand the relationships he established and how he handled his clients in such a professional manner and really always went above and beyond to make sure that his clients were well taken care of, I could not have had a better mentor than my father. Witnessing that, of course I wanted to follow in his footsteps. Growing up, he said, "You know, you really should get into real estate." Of course, most kids take their own direction, which I did initially.

I started as an entrepreneur and started my own business. Previously, as a model and actress, I started a modeling and talent agency that grew beyond my wildest expectations to over 500 models and actors. Then, eventually, when my daughter came along, I sold it and was a consultant for the business. At that point, my dad's like, "Okay, now's the time for you to get into real estate," because I had a non-compete contract with the business that I sold. I thought, "Okay, perfect timing." My daughter was old enough for me to really get involved in real estate.

When I got my license in July of 2005, I quickly realized I had clients standing in line and I was still waiting for my license to come in the mail. Fortunately for me, I had a nice sphere of influence, having been a native Californian and understanding the principles of building a business and fostering relationships and being a shrewd negotiator, a skill I had developed when running my first business. I also understood that being a master at creative and strategic marketing was critical. Because it doesn't do any good if nobody knows you have a business. Then they can't do business with you.

For me, out the gate I had clients standing by. My business took off. I was Rookie of the Year. Then I told my first broker, "Listen, I am going to be a top producer." She said, "I don't doubt that." Because my dad was scaling down at that point. Within 2-and-a-half years I was the top producer of Century 21. I recall my father and my mother being at the award ceremony and it was such a special occasion because my dad, and my mom of course, was so proud of me, that not only had I met, but exceeded his expectations of me working in real estate.

I also took pride in carrying on the traditions of how he built his business, which really is client care and providing the highest level of extraordinary service for clients. I would always tell my dad, "Dad, we get all these hard transactions, the kind that typically fall apart for most realtors," and he said, "That's because you're tenacious and persistent, and because of that," he said, "you always manage to keep it all together and close it successfully." It is interesting. Throughout the course of my real estate career, my broker has even said, "Kathleen, I can't even believe you always get transactions with things and issues that I've never seen in 40 years."

Ultimately, I think that being a good problem solver is key to my success, as well, because I always figure out a way to fix a problem. Whatever the problem is, I fix it. I think my clients appreciate that because they see firsthand, because they've got a front row seat to all the issues that can arise in a transaction, which many times are beyond anybody's realization or expectation. They see how I handle each, one at a time, and then somehow we cross the finish line and successfully close that transaction.

I do believe that for each and every client, I look at what their needs, desires, and goals are and I genuinely care about their best interest, whatever it might be. In some cases, I've loaned them money to get the house painted so that they can get top dollar. I do free staging because it enhances the value. I try to set myself apart with what I do and how I do it for my clients. They clearly see that all realtors are not created equal and that the level of service they get is uncompromising, of which the end result for them, if they're selling a house, is top dollar, and if they're a buyer, then they see that I go above and beyond, sometimes for homes that are overpriced by $100,000.

I help educate the seller through their agent, who has overpriced the home because they're not good at actually determining price on the house or have listed it too high just to garner the listing in the first place. When submitting an offer, it may appear as a low ball offer, but with how it's packaged, with a cover letter, with a detailed analysis of the value and a little bit about my buyer, I can usually get the seller to reevaluate and change their perception of the value of their own house and drop the price $100,000. In turn, I can do the same thing on the listing side. I change buyers' perception of value, where they may come in low, and then I help them increase that perception of value so that my sellers get a higher price.

What personal attributes, traits, or qualities have most contributed to your success? How did you develop these?

I think first and foremost it's realizing that each client has their own set of needs. For me, I love to analyze things. I analyze my clients, what their needs and goals are, because you may have someone who has a sense of urgency to sell the home, and if they have a sense of urgency, then whatever their needs, goals, and desires are, I adopt those. I implement a plan.

I always ask my clients, "Hey, did you play sports?" Of course, most of the time they'll say, "Yes." I say, "Okay, so when you played sports, you probably never went into a game without a game plan, right?" Of course, they acknowledge, "Yes." I say, "Well, it's the same thing that I like to do in real estate. I played sports growing up so my mind is kind of wired differently than maybe someone who hasn't." Especially considering that, when I grew up, not as many women were playing sports as they do today. Having two brothers, I think it gave me a strategic advantage to look at things differently.

When I go in, I analyze everything about the house. I analyze my clients, their motivation for selling, what their needs and desires are, what their personality type is because if you're dealing with an engineer, then they're very detail-oriented and they're all about the numbers and they're going to read every word in the contract. I have to adapt to my clients, who they are, how they are, and what their needs are. That way, when I create a game plan for them specifically, for them personally, as well as what I'm going to do for their house, the end result is exactly what they want. So, I've either met and/or exceeded their expectations.

There was one instance that is a perfect example of what I'm saying. A former client had referred me to an associate. He was a detective in a police department. He was going to be retiring. He was whining and complaining at the office that he'd interviewed five realtors. He didn't like any of them. My former client said, "Oh, by the way, you should contact my realtor. If she can put up with me, I'm sure she can put up with you." Because he was a tough cookie. He called me up and I met with him and his wife and he clearly told me he had utilized five realtors in the past and hated them all, that he never trusted them. He pounded his hand on the table and said, "What are you going to do if I want to fire you?" I said, "Well, that's never happened and you're not going to be the first."

I said, "Just let me know what your goals and desires are and I will make it happen." He told me, "I want to close Escrow. I want this house sold. I want to close by August 18th and I want this amount of money. This is my bottom line." I said, "Okay. I'll make that happen." "In the interim," I said, "I will change your perception on realtors."

I went to work. I staged the house for free and showcased it. I always do professional pictures to harness the power of the internet. I create a personal website for my clients so the address is 123mainstreet.com or whatever the address is. I'm big on marketing. When we got the offers in we had a few hiccups and we were able to overcome those. When we opened Escrow, everything was going along fine.

Then, of course, towards the end he had a run in with the homeowner's association individual that drives around to see if there's anything wrong with your house. Of course, they took it as an opportunity to flag it for something: trim the tree, paint the fascia. The wife told me. "Oh, Kathleen," she says, "If he sees this, he's not going to want to sell the house now, just for spite because he doesn't like this person." I say, "Well, let's not tell him. Let me get my tree trimmer over there and trim the tree and I'll pay the termite guy extra. I'll pay him to paint the fascia. Then we've solved the problem." Because I could see her eyes were glazing over. We were almost to the finish line. I wanted to make sure nothing got in the way of that.

We closed Escrow. He had no idea what had transpired. Then he was thrilled that we actually closed on the day that he wanted to close. He got more money than he thought he would get. He couldn't believe it. I did in fact change his perception of realtors, so much so that when they were moving to Colorado and they got there, he quickly realized he didn't like any of the realtors there, so he called me up and said, "Kathleen, why are you not here in Colorado? We need you." I said, "Well, I'm here in California, but I'll be your consultant. I'm standing by if you have any questions or concerns with any of your real estate transactions in Colorado. Feel free to call me."

He was good with that. I walked him through his contracts and everything else there so he felt like he really had someone looking out for his best interest, which is what clients really want at the end of the day.

What were some of the major adversities and trials you had to overcome to achieve your goals?

I think the biggest challenge was getting my short sale specialist certification and dealing with when the real estate market turned upside down, the height of the market being 2006, 2007, and 2008. Of course, 2008 was the beginning of the recession. When the market was shifting, I saw a lot of realtors exiting because suddenly houses didn't sell themselves anymore and consequently it took a lot of hard work. Well, I was never opposed to hard work. In fact, it's kind of how I grew up, the way our family was. It's the way my father was with the work ethic he had. It just was second nature to me.

Consequently, I immediately went ahead and got my short sale certification because I thought, "What are you going to do, just help your clients in the good times and not help them in the challenging times?" You need to be there if you're truly committed to helping your clients and their real estate needs, whatever they might be, and not just because it's easy. Consequently, when I got certified to do short sales, I immediately realized that the banks weren't really set up, so it was an uphill battle. You could work two to three years on a short sale and it was very labor-intensive.

But I am tenacious and persistent, and in spite of all the red tape and all the challenges that the banks had in the beginning, I prevailed. You see, the banks weren't set up to take homes back. They were set up to provide loans and move on. Consequently, it made it very challenging, not only for the homeowners, who certainly all wanted to keep their homes, but for the realtor, as well. I was sad to see how many homeowners were losing their homes, some because they used their homes as an ATM machine and others because they were just a victim of circumstance, such as predatory lending.

There are two clients in particular that I was able to help go against the banks and one in particular I helped go against some unscrupulous realtors that were trying to steal their house. In these situations, I swooped in and saved the day. In fact, they call me Super Realtor. They were going to get me a little cape with an "SR" on it because I swooped in and was able to save their homes. To this day, they call me their real estate angel because they know without a shadow of a doubt that if I hadn't basically been a whistleblower and gone up against these people, which is not easy to do, they would have lost their homes. It was like me going up against Goliath.

That's the conviction I got from my father, that you fight for what's right. You just don't roll over. You don't walk away if something's not easy. You hang in there. You walk through the fire. You do whatever you have to do to help your client. It's not about selling homes and it's not just about helping buyers buy homes. In these cases, I was able to help people save their homes. When your home is your haven, it's your sanctuary in the world. There isn't anything more important to me than knowing that I was able to make a difference in those homeowners' lives, to save their homes.

For example, last year there was an instance where the homeowner wanted to hire this male realtor to list the house and he wanted to have me help them buy a house. Well, 18 months went by, and of course, he didn't sell the house. It backed up to a busy street. Beautiful home, but backing up to a busy street certainly deters a lot of prospective buyers. Of course, I always have a plan around the location if there's an issue such as that.

Of course, I sat quietly waiting. Then, when 18 months had passed, I got the call and I met with the homeowners to list the house because the other guy couldn't sell it. Now I would have the opportunity to help them list it and purchase another home. I found out that in that past 18 months he had lost his job. I asked, "Are you still in your severance package?" He said, "No, we're into our savings." I thought, "Wow. Here's a family with four children, two dogs, and he's passed his severance. They don't have any income whatsoever and they're going to lose this house if we don't do something."

I had to assess their situation, which clearly was a sense of urgency, and this other guy couldn't sell the house in 18 months. I certainly am not the type of realtor who comes in and just slashes the price. In fact, I do the opposite of that because I protect a client's bottom line. There's nothing more important than me looking their bottom line that as if it's my own bottom line. Clients appreciate that.

They had a 14,000 square foot lot. I told them, "Part of your yard needs to be fixed up. Half of your yard is like a green screen with beautiful plants that come up over the fence so you can't actually see the cars driving by, but the other half doesn't have that green screen. From your beautiful master bedroom you see all the cars driving by, dump trucks, this and that, because there's construction going on up the road." I said, "Out of sight, out of mind. If you fill in that green screen, you'll see that buyers won't notice it as much. It won't bother them because they don't see it when they're inside the house."

He did exactly what I said and filled it in and he said, "I don't know why I didn't do that sooner. It always bothered me when I would look out my bedroom or bathroom window and see the cars driving by. It would always bother me." I said, "Well, if it bothers you, you can imagine it's going to bother a prospective buyer." We were priced at 1.65 on the house, so it's a pretty big price point. I told him, "Listen, we have to hit this out of the ball park. I'm going to create a marketing plan specific to driving buyers and creating a buyer frenzy."

This was in January. Of course, selling a home in January isn't easy. People are still getting over the expense of Christmas, so there aren't a lot of buyers lined up to buy homes in January. My whole marketing theme around bringing buyers to this house in was to take drone photos, which created the money shot. They were spectacular photos, which something I pride myself on. I understand that you have to create the visual desire so that when buyers see it they fall in love with it and they can't resist coming to the house to see it.

I created this whole ad campaign around, "If your New Year's resolution is to find your dream home, well here it is," with the money shot, the aerial shots, and the interior shots, for which I staged the house. It looked like a model home. I had a catered open house on Sunday. Every time I had to wait a week because I wanted to get everything built up. Then I did two half-page ads in the LA Times, the Orange County paper, and put it throughout the internet. We had so many people there. I did exactly what I had hoped to do, create the buyer frenzy. We got an offer from an attorney that night and other offers that came in. They got exactly what they wanted price-wise and we closed Escrow in 30 days.

That's a perfect example of how another realtor had it for 18 months and couldn't sell it and then I came in and assessed the fact that there was a sense of urgency. Normally, I'll roll out marketing. In this case I had to throw it all at the wall at once, but I did it strategically, in a way to drive as many buyers as I could at once so they would all compete against each other. The end result was nothing short of magical for my clients because they were absolutely thrilled we got them out from under that house. Then, when he got another job, I was able to get them into another house.

This is the kind of thing my clients get. It's not just about the relationships, but it creates almost a fan club because they realize that I have a skill set that is above and beyond what a lot of average realtors will do for their clients. I don't have a problem spending the money on full-on advertising to really showcase their house and get the word out there to make sure we accomplish their real estate goals and get them top dollar.

What is your vision for your career for the next five years?

Well, ideally I feel like the next step would be become a broker. My dad was a real estate broker. I've just been so busy selling real estate, which I feel so grateful to be able to do successfully because I've genuinely put my client's best interests at heart. I don't even ever worry about a commission check, I don't even focus on that, and the abundance just comes. Consequently, the next step would be to get my brokers' license, which I'm working on right now, and eventually open up my own realty company and to continue to do what I do.

I do love mentoring agents. I would really like to be able to continue to help other agents understand the fundamentals of how to be successful in real estate. It's not how much you sell that is important at the end of the day; it's really how well you do what you do. When you go above and beyond and provide the highest level of extraordinary service, when you pull out all the stops for any client, whatever that might be, to make things happen for them, you will have a successful career. You understand the importance of fostering and valuing those relationships and taking great care of those clients.

What do you feel is the best way you market yourself as a real estate professional for continual growth?

Well, what's interesting is when you create a great reputation and a following, it kind of feeds itself. I also find that the accolades I receive each year in Orange Coast Magazine continue to perpetuate the reputation I've established, how I've set myself apart, how my philosophy on real estate is set apart from my competition. It doesn't cost a homeowner or a prospective buyer anything. It really doesn't cost them any more to have the best real estate professional in Orange County.

I was recently asked to be a guest speaker at Chapman University in the city of Orange and they asked me to speak on home buyers avoiding costly mistakes. The two sessions I had were packed, just packed. Standing room only. Nobody wants to make mistakes in life and certainly not costly ones. When it comes to real estate, you're in jeopardy of making some seriously costly mistakes. I told them first and foremost that the realtor you choose is so important and all realtors are not created equal. If you're not interviewing several realtors to find out everything about them, you are taking a big risk.

I said, "Nobody even asks these realtors if they're good negotiators." It's such an integral part of what a realtor does. I said, "If you're a buyer and you're trying to get a house and you've got a realtor who's not a good negotiator, how many homes are you going to lose out on before you actually get one? At that point, it's probably not your top choice." One lady raised her hand. She said, "Yeah, my realtor wasn't a good negotiator. We submitted ten different offers on ten different houses. I didn't get any of them." I said, "Well, there's a perfect example for you." It's frustrating because, again, if that realtor isn't savvy enough to understand how to negotiate and how to get an offer accepted and how to set your offer apart from the other offers on the table, then they are going to have a hard time getting a house.

I also talked about home inspectors. In the state of California, you don't have to be licensed to be a home inspector and that's a problem in and of itself. I said, "For my clients, the condition of a home affects the value, so if there's something wrong with the condition you can bet that we're going to renegotiate the value of that home or ask for credit. You can't do that if you don't have a good inspector to really undermine the house and determine what's wrong with the house so you can then bring that to their attention and renegotiate it."

With that, I told them, "My home inspector is a general contractor. He's also licensed to do mold inspection and for pool and spa inspections. He's like 3-in-1. Nobody knows a house better than him, because he's built homes before. You don't want someone who just has a certification they spent $250 for to inspect homes and get a matching hat and shirt and a "Here's your software."

A lady raised her hand and said, "Yeah. My realtor had one of those. The lady that came to do the inspection said, 'Yeah, I'm a bartender, but I just got my certification. I paid $250 for it, so now I'm doing home inspections.'" I told my realtor, "Well, that's kind of scary, if she's a bartender. She just got her certification for home inspections. I'd probably rather have that lady making me a martini versus inspecting a home."

I helped the individuals that attended my class to understand that you have to do your due diligence to find a top-notch realtor and nothing less should ever be accepted. Then that realtor will have a top-notch home inspector to protect your potential investment when you purchase a house.

What's the biggest misconception/myth that people have about working with a real estate agent?

I think the biggest misconception is people don't realize all of what realtors do, even if you narrow it down and get somebody who's really, really good at what they do. It's like the cartoon character, Felix the Cat. He had his little bag of tricks, so to speak. You need to have a lot going on in your bag of tricks because you are going to need to be able to problem solve and really understand the market, understand the value of a home, not only pricing it for a client, pricing it appropriately. Pricing a home is an art. Not everybody knows how to price it. They price it too high. Certainly, if it's too low, that's not good for the client. Then, if you're representing the buyer, you need to help them understand the pricing.

The biggest thing I find is managing a client's expectations and their emotions and helping them change their perception as necessary. If they're fixated on something small, help them see the big picture of a home they're purchasing, and/or if a seller's selling the home, help them see the big picture and change their perception of value. If they're attached to a price because a home up the street sold for $100,000 more it's like, "Yeah, and that house had a pool and it was highly upgraded and yours isn't." A lot of times it's really just educating the client. I believe that the only way that people can make informed decisions is if they have the information.

If you were to get a call from a family member in another state wanting to sell their home, what advice would you give them about selecting an agent who can best serve their needs?

I think the most important thing to do when looking for a realtor is to create a list of questions and think about interviewing them. The questions on that interview list should include, first and foremost, "How long have you been selling real estate? What sets you apart as a real estate professional from your competition? Share some examples with me."

If someone is interviewing a realtor as a buyer, then the question would be, "Share with me some past stories of client success where you felt your negotiating skills helped your buyer get the house over somebody else. What are some of your strategic plans that you will put into place to get my offer accepted over other people's offers? Tell me about your home inspector. What are their qualifications? Are they a general contractor? Are they licensed to inspect mold? Will they test for mold when they're there? Are they experienced at inspecting a pool or a spa if there's a pool or a spa there?"

These are some of the questions that you can ask someone in order to have a better understanding of their skill set is. There are different questions if you're a prospective seller. The first questions would be the same, of course. "How long have you been in real estate? Tell me about some of your recent sales. How close was the sales price to the list price? Will you create a marketing plan for me that is very specific as to what you will be doing to market and advertise my home? What's your budget for that?"

The thing is that sometimes people want to negotiate the commission. What they forget is that if somebody can't even negotiate their commissions and they want to just give it away, do it for the lowest amount possible, how are they going to negotiate the sale of your house and get you top dollar? They're going to be more interested in selling it quickly and dropping the price. Typically, the type of realtors that reduce in price are the type that just stick a sign in the yard and sell the house quickly so they can move onto the next one. They're not as concerned about the client's bottom line; they're more concerned about their commission check. Consequently, that's not a good scenario.

More important for a prospective seller to understand is that in negotiating, you need to have someone who's a shrewd negotiator. Then they can change the buyer's perception of value so the buyer is willing to pay more money for that house. That's worth its weight in gold because then you end up getting top dollar for your house. Any reduction in commission would have been minor compared to what you garner financially by having a really skilled negotiator as a listing agent. Having them share those stories with you is important so you see firsthand what they did? Do they stage the home? Do they use a professional photographer?

It's kind of scary today with everything online. All the buyers are very savvy because all the information about the homes is online. Zillow has their values on there, which aren't necessarily always accurate. Nonetheless, people might use that as a gauge. For realtors who are using their camera on their phone to take pictures, it's not good enough, you know? Then they want a big commission. For me, that is just not professional. Every client selling their home deserves to have professional photos of their house, showcasing it online, because if somebody's looking at pictures and the pictures are full of shadows and dark and you can't really tell what the room looks like or any defining features in it, that makes a big difference.

I had a situation recently where someone fired their realtor because they were completely uncomfortable with how the transaction was being handled. The listing was on the market for 45 days. I have a client across the street who loves and adores me and told this person, "Oh, you need to call Kathleen. She'll help you." She canceled that contract. I looked at the pictures from the other realtor and I thought, "Wow." The pictures weren't very good. when I take photos of a house, I'll go room by room and showcase each room. If there's too much furniture in the room, well, we'll just move it out.

I said, "I would suggest painting your kitchen cabinets white." They were a very dark brown. The home was built in 1960, so those were original cabinets. I said, "They'll look a lot nicer and newer and more modern if you paint them white. Everybody loves white cabinets now."

She did exactly that. She painted the cabinets white. She called and she says, "Kathleen, I absolutely love my new kitchen." She goes, "It feels brand-new." I said, "Exactly." I went in and took professional photos. It looked like a different house. You wouldn't even have known it was the same house.

Here's a house that had been on the market for 45 days. She had already bought a house, also in Colorado. She had a sense of urgency because now she had two houses. Within one week, less than a week actually, we got the first offer, and then the second offer came in on the heels of that one. It was actually someone who used to live in California, had moved to Texas and didn't like Texas, and wanted to come back to California. They saw the photos, fell in love with it. It kind of reminded them of the house that they had sold. They came in at a full price offer.

If she had stuck with the other agent, who wanted to quickly drop the price from 729 to 699 she would have lost out. That's a substantial amount of money out of that poor seller's pocket and she's retired, so every penny matters to her. She had lost her husband. I came in, made a few changes. She painted the kitchen the cabinets, which made all the difference in the world, and she got exactly what she was asking, 729. She was calling me her guardian angel. She's like, "I'm just over the moon with you, Kathleen. I couldn't be happier." The end result for her was it was in Escrow now and wed be closing soon and she'd be able to move to Colorado. She had a great experience.

How can someone that needs a real estate agent find out more about you and how you can help?

They can go to my website at www.gowithmonroe.com. or call me at 949-702-1955.

Top Agent Robyne Roveccio

Robyne is an Associate Broker with Realty ONE Group, where she prides herself on exceeding her customers' expectations in the purchase and sale of residential real estate. It's important to her that her clients know, like, and trust her, and she works to that end. She works by referral only and enjoys celebrating the client she serves by supporting their businesses through quarterly business mixers and client appreciation parties.

She holds a Bachelor's degree in education, a Master's degree in counseling, and an Arizona real estate broker's license. Her proudest moments include being one of 16 recipients of the Silver Apple Award for teaching excellence, being named Top Agent Magazine's top agent for August 2015, and being in the top 20 of the most successful agents in her Realty ONE Group office in 2015.

In addition to her highly successful real estate career, Robyne competed nationally for eight years and earned her IFBB Figure Pro card in 2013.

What led you to real estate? Was it something you always knew you wanted to do?

Being a real estate agent is something I never intended to become. I was working in public education as a teacher and a counselor for about 15 years and was five years overdue for a change. There was a freeze on education salaries and I was doing more paperwork than helping kids, which is what I really love to do. I was considering going back to school to get my PhD in either psychology or education administration because it seemed like the logical thing to do, the next step in my career.

A friend of mine had just graduated from real estate school. She was working from home and making a decent living. So, with no knowledge of the industry, but a huge desire to be doing anything other than what I was doing, in 2005 I became a Realtor.

I had this perception about being a salesperson and I thought, "Sales is not my strong suit." That's just kind of funny, looking back compared to where I am now. I don't sell real estate, I build relationships with people who have houses to buy and sell.

What personal attributes, traits, or qualities have most contributed to your success and how did you develop these?

I'd have to say the attributes that contributed to my success were primarily perseverance; a deep, deep love of helping people; a thirst for

110

knowledge; being extremely disciplined; and being okay with not being successful right out of the gate, learning to fail forward and be patient with my progress. I think those were the most contributing factors to my success.

The second part of your question, how did I develop these traits? I think my deep love for helping people is just part of who I am and it's the fiber of my being. I've always been in the helping profession. I have always loved being of service to people. Perseverance, discipline, and failing forward, I attribute these to two things. One is, as a teenager, I dropped out of high school in the middle of my junior year and had to go to work full-time. I left home at an early age to work and live on my own. It took a lot of perseverance, it took a lot of discipline, and it took a lot of hard work to stay afloat. I think I gained an incredible understanding what I was really capable of. Because at 16, 17 years old, you're not really quite sure what you're capable of. I threw myself into the situation and I came out on top. I think that that's where I got the qualities to succeed.

Another way I developed perseverance and discipline was during my years as a competitive athlete. When I set a goal to get my pro card, I just knew that I was going to get it. There was nothing stopping me or that was going to get in my way. I didn't care how long it took. I didn't care what I had to do to get it done, as far as changing my training, modifying my diet, etc. I just persevered. I took the lessons I learned as a teen and I knew I would find a way to succeed. I just kept moving forward and eventually it happened.

Can you give specific examples of when these traits have played a role in your path toward success?

Sure. Much like my training as a competitive athlete, I happened to choose perfect times to get to real estate when the market was tanking. Having the mindset that I wasn't a salesperson and not having a steady paycheck coming in, as I had had in the 16 years, I was in public education. I was thinking, "Okay, well, I've been here before, where things have been really hard, and it seems like a monumental wall to climb over. However, I have gained a lot of evidence that I can persevere, and if I stay focused and I stay disciplined and I set goals, I can build a business I can depend on."

What were some of the major adversities and trials you had to overcome to achieve your goals?

That's a great question. As I said, I got into real estate during the worst market ever. This is a time when real estate agents were quitting and going back to full-time jobs. The industry was turned upside down. I really had to, with the limited knowledge I had of the real estate industry, find a way to build my business, build my clientele, and learn from the ground up.

Not having any client base at all, people knew me as an educator, not as a real estate agent, I found a niche in For Sale by Owners. There were a lot of people trying to sell their homes by themselves at the time. I just tapped into what I knew and who I was. I knew I loved to help

112

people and I knew I loved to teach people. So, I would meet with For Sale by Owners, I would give them the tools they needed to sell their home and developed a relationship with them. I tapped into what I knew I was good at and applied it to the real estate business. Most For Sale by Owners would eventually list with me, then they would tell their friends and my business just grew from there.

Along the way, I earned a few designations and became very educated in the inner workings of the real estate industry very quickly. That was one way I overcame that major tank in the real estate industry and just branded myself as somebody who would be long-term in the industry in terms of building a great relationship with people.

Some of those clients are still clients today, which is really cool. For me, real estate is all about the relationship. I can't remember who said this, but people don't care how much you know until they know how much you care and real estate really isn't any different. There was a time when I really didn't know if real estate was for me because I didn't like to do the things that coaches tell you to do, like door knock and cold call. I really had to dig deep and say, "How can I make this business something that I am passionate about and I love to do every day?" It's really knowing who you are and knowing what you love to do. I crafted the business around my highest values, which are being a helper and creating lasting relationships.

What kept you going despite these obstacles? Why didn't you give up?

I have a "failure is not an option" mentality. I have a lot of patience. In my past careers I've had as an educator, in administration, in all of that, I knew that I had to take my lumps, per se, and I knew that there was an evolution to this and that I would fail forward. I have a really great relationship with failure. I also had a lot of evidence that I can succeed based on my being a competitive athlete and being a young teen on my own. I just had a lot of evidence that I can succeed in the most adverse conditions, and I truly believe that there's always a solution to obstacles. The solution may not look like I want it to, but the end result is what's important.

What is your vision for your career for the next five years?

I'm kind of entering a new phase of my real estate career. I'm building a team right now. That includes hiring full-time admin and buyers agents and maybe a listing agent. But my true passion, as you've heard throughout this whole interview, is that I want to help people. My vision for the next five years is to leave the industry better than I found it. I'm developing a program for real estate agents that will serve to increase the level of care they provide to the public and give them the tools that will assist them in growing their business and becoming successful realtors themselves.

The National Association of Realtors comes out with what's called a Danger Report and one of the key points is that real estate agents need to be better practitioners and serve the public better because the public doesn't have a great perception of who we are. My goal for the next five years is to implement this program and leave the industry at some point better than I found it.

What do you feel is the best way you market yourself as a real estate professional for continual growth?

That's a great question and I really hope the readers out there who are real estate agents hear this. Just really be authentic, be consistent, and be prepared. Being authentic really requires you to do some soul searching as far as how you want to run your business. As I've mentioned, I've been able to craft the business that matches my style. This may not be the style for other people, but I just love the relationship and people know that. My clients know that. It's all about helping people get to the end result, which is called selling or buying a house.

That's just how I market myself and that's why I work by referral only. I had 91% of my clients last year as referrals. I do get some other through signs, calls, things like that, but that's how I grow my business.

What's the biggest misconception/myth that people have about working with a real estate agent?

I would say it's that our efforts are not in direct proportion to our compensation. Again, coming from a background of working with For Sale By Owners, for the majority of For Sale By Owner's, the only reason they want to sell their house on their own is to not pay a commission. There are so many things that the public just doesn't understand. From the time we hold the buyer and seller consultation to the close of Escrow and beyond, there is no less than 20 people involved in that transaction and dozens of documents and mounds of paperwork. It's my job to know the contract inside and out, make sure the process is as seamless as possible, and keep the transaction in compliance with what the parties agreed to.

Arizona is one of the few states where we can write the contract and that's a huge responsibility. That would be another thing I would want real estate readers to really understand, that it is a huge responsibility to write that contract for your clients. It's a lot of liability on our part, as well. I think that sometimes people don't understand what is involved in the contract-to-close process.

I go to a lot of continuing education classes that are taught by attorneys and the top people in the field like the icon Bill Gray. My job is to keep my clients in compliance with the terms of their contract and also help them make a very important financial decision. I'm a very careful practitioner.

If you were to get a call from a family member in another state wanting to sell their home, what advice would you give them about selecting an agent who can best serve their needs?

If someone, either a family member or a friend, was coming from out of state, I would have them, if they could, rent for a few months. I'm not sure if you're familiar with Arizona, but we have a very diverse landscape here. Maricopa County has a lot of niche neighborhoods. I would want them to drive around some neighborhoods, find out where they would like to be, what's most valuable to them. Do they like to be up in the mountains? Do they like to be in urban areas? Do they like a lot of land? There's just so much to choose from here. If they could rent for a little while, that would be great.

Then, most definitely, interviewing no fewer than three agents. Sometimes it's not great to have a family member as your client because it's hard for them to fire you. They feel stuck and you never want the client to feel stuck. I would say interview at least three agents, look at how many properties they've sold, how many transactions they've been through. The average real estate agent now only does a couple of transactions a year. Make sure the person you've hired really has some expertise in your market area and also in transactions.

How can someone that needs a real estate agent find out more about you and how you can help?

They can go to my website at RobyneRoveccio.com or email me at robyne@robyneroveccio.com. I would be happy to sit down with them, have a buyer consultation or a seller consultation. I want them to grill me. I want them to be very comfortable with their choice in hiring me as their real estate agent. I like to meet with them face to face. It's not like, "Just call me and I'll put you in my car and we'll go for a ride." It has to be a good fit for both of us, and I want to make sure I can meet your expectations and not give you something that's unrealistic.

Top Agent Tami Gosselin

Tami Gosselin is with Century 21 M&M Associates, based out of Modesto, California. Having been in real estate since 2002, Tami is in the top 1% nationwide. Twelve-time consecutive Centurion Award-winner and Honor Society Award-winner ranked in the top 500 for real estate marketers in 2014. In 2015, USAA certified, Cendant certified, certified distressed property expert, RES.net certified, and Equator platinum certified. She also has two consecutive years as the number one agent, 2009 and 2010, and then the number three agent in 2012 in the US for American Home Shield home warranty protection. Tami is ranked in the top 1,000 for homes sold in 2013 and 2014 in the US and she is determined to help her clients by being a source of information. She knows that relocating a family from as far as another country and as near as across the street has the potential to be either the best decision you made in years or a stressful one.

Her focus is in the experience because she understands the complexities of buying and selling homes. She wants her clients to have the kind of experience that breeds sustained relationships and clients for life.

What led you to real estate? Was it something you always knew you wanted to do?

No, actually it was back when I was only 21 years old. My husband was selling the first property he had ever purchased and the real estate agent said, "You know, you'd make a great real estate agent," and that always stuck with me. When I became pregnant with my first child, my husband said, "Why don't you get your real estate license?" So I did and here I am.

What personal attributes, traits, or qualities have most contributed to your success? How did you develop these?

I think personality and being a people-person is huge in this industry. Also, I've learned over the years through coaching to become a chameleon and mirror and match the person you're working with. If they talk fast, I talk fast. If they talk slow, I talk slow. You want to make whoever you're working with feel very comfortable when you're around them. Then, my personal attributes are that I'm extremely self-disciplined and an organized person and committed to executing the daily activities necessary to continue growing my business at a high level. I also have a bubbly personality. I enjoy making people's dreams become a reality.

I got my real estate license when I was 24 years old. I knew nothing about real estate when I got my license, so I joined a coaching company 45 days after I got my license. All I've ever done is exactly what they told me to do and I sold 40 homes my first year.

Can you give specific examples of when these traits have played a role in your path toward success?

I think it's just being consistent and setting goals. Every year, I put together a business plan. I set a yearly goal, I set a daily goal, I set a weekly goal, I set a monthly goal, and I set a quarterly goal. I review those goals daily, weekly, monthly, quarterly, depending on what I'm working, whether it's my listing goal or my buyers-under-contract goal or my number-of-closings goal. I post my goals on my wall in front of me, next to my computer, so it's in front of me at all times. In my daily business, I'm rewarded every day with new clients, referrals from past clients, and agents across the nation because I'm constantly keeping in contact with everyone. I am also asked frequently to mentor agents throughout the year and I find giving back extremely rewarding. I love to give back. I love helping agents, whether they're a new agent or a seasoned agent, teaching them how they can take their business to the next level.

Let's just say my goal is to reach out to 20 people a day and I hit that goal by noon. That doesn't mean that I'm done for the day. That just means that I can work harder to get ahead of my numbers for the week.

Most people think, "Okay, I hit my goal for the day. I can go home." No, no, no. I don't go home; I keep plugging forward. Now let's just say it's five o'clock and I haven't hit my number. That doesn't mean I get to go home either. I'll stay here until seven, eight, nine o'clock at night until I hit that goal. I do not leave my office until I've hit my goal every day.

What were some of the major adversities and trials that you had to overcome to achieve your goals?

There's a huge amount of sacrifice in this industry to hit the goals I hit every year. There are times when I miss my kids' games, miss different events, because I'm a goal-oriented type of person and if I don't hit my goals, I'm staying here until I hit my goals. That's been a huge sacrifice in order to hit my goals every single year. There are things I have to give up to be able to do that.

What kept you going despite these obstacles? Why didn't you give up?

It's because I want to be able to retire at a young age. I'm 38 years old. I set a goal at 24 that I will retire by the age of 45. That's what I focus on, that I'm going to able to enjoy my kids at a young age versus working to the age of 65. That's what keeps me going. I stay focused on that number, that age of 45, and I have to hit certain goals every single year to be able to achieve that. That's what keeps me focused.

What is your vision for your career for the next five years?

I started a new plan actually. I've been out here in California working in this area for 14 years and I conquered it out here. Now, I'm getting my real estate license out in Florida. I work for Century 21 here in California, so I know how the Century 21 system works. I love it, so I'm going to start working for a Century 21 company out in Boca Raton, Florida. I'm going to implement all the tools that I've implemented out here for success in California out in Florida. I'm super excited about this because that's where my family is going to retire. I've looked at Florida as a retirement place for many years, so I want to implement that now, since I have seven years left to really build a big business out there and have both my business in Florida, as well as California, running smoothly by the time that I retire. Then my team will just be producing my business during my retirement years.

My goal is to interact one week a month between both businesses. That's my goal when I retire, just to take care of the hard stuff, where you have to think outside of the box. There are a lot of big obstacles to overcome at times, and with my experience, I've sold over 1,500 homes during my career of 14 years. I'm able to overcome most obstacles with my experience. I don't feel there's any obstacle too big because there's a solution for everything.

What do you feel is the best way you market yourself as a real estate professional for continual growth?

It's staying in touch with my past clients, friends, and family every single year. I hand-write and personally sign my Christmas cards and add a calendar with them that goes out to my entire database. They key to a successful Christmas card is to mail it the day after Thanksgiving. Mine is the first Christmas card that everyone in my database gets. As they move my Christmas card around their house, my face is in front of them, my name is in front of them. Also, I send out monthly postcards to my entire database. Quarterly mailing, and when I say 'quarterly', it means giving them something of value whether it be a pen, a chip clip, a key chain, or a notepad. I give them something of value to remind them of me every quarter. I also talk to them. I have my A-clients and B-clients. Talking to my A-clients, whether it's monthly or quarterly, and my B-clients bi-yearly. With staying in touch, being in front of my entire database all the time, that's allowed me to continually grow my business.

What's the biggest misconception/myth that people have about working with a real estate agent?

Most people feel that most real estate agents are overpaid and under-worked because they think that it's just putting a sign in the yard, signing a few documents, putting your house on the internet, and bam! It's sold. Oh my goodness, it's so much more than that. There's so much that even goes into the preparation of putting a home on the market or

124

all the time out showing a buyer a property and making multiple offers. A lot people think that when getting a real estate license, the money's just going to flow in, the clients are just going to magically come in, the phones are just going to start ringing. No, not at all.

There's also a lot of training that is involved after getting your license. There is definitely a ton of business out there, but you have to work for it. The second I take a listing my seller knows my listing plan of action. On every appointment I go on, whether it's a buyer or a listing, I have a plan of action in place so my clients always know where we are at throughout the entire process. I've never been told that I'm overpaid and under-worked because I always bring value to the table on every transaction. All you readers out there, if you want to get your real estate license, great. It's a wonderful business to be in, but there is a lot of hard work.

There is a lot of behind-the-scenes that goes into every transaction, many, many hours of hard work and thinking outside the box to put together multiple transactions. I've had a transaction that depends on five different transactions to close and it's a domino effect. Just trying to juggle all of that is huge, making sure we're all on our time frames and everything falls into place.

If you were to get a call from a family member in another state wanting to sell their home, what advice would you give them about selecting an agent who can best serve their needs?

I have a listing plan of action that I have in place for every listing I take. My advice to them would be definitely to interview three agents and see what they're going to do for them. On every listing I take, I meet with my clients multiple times before we actually put the house on the market. I stage all my properties. You can hire a staging company, but I go through the property and I stage it, I de-clutter it. I want it to be perfect when I have my professional photographer come out and take all my photos.

That would be my advice to my friend or family member that's reaching out to me on who they are going to pick. What they need is an agent who is going to hold their hand and show them what they need to do to first get it ready to put it on the market, then the steps that they're going to take during the sale of the property. I want to make sure they're going to hire a professional photographer to take their photos. If the regional area is big on open houses, hold open houses. Hold the broker open. I would give them all the advice of what it takes to get a property sold out here and I would check to see what agents do in that area. I would Google their address, go to Zillow, check out some of the properties in that area to see what agents are doing. Then I would help them. I would definitely give them a lending hand on interviewing the agents for them.

How can someone who needs a real estate agent find out more about you and how you can help?

You can definitely Google me. I have my personal website which is TamiGosselin.com. It has my personal bio on there. Also, Zillow.com has another web page about me and it goes over my current listings and some of my past sales. I have a video with American Home Shield that states I will provide a home warranty on every one of my transactions, whether the seller pays for it or not. I'm a big advocate for home warranties. In the first year, it gives the buyer a peace of mind. Let's just say you move in today and in 30 days your heater or air conditioner goes out. You call the home warranty company, you pay a service fee $60 or $70, and they come out and repair or replace. That's the best way to find out about me, if you don't know me personally.

Top Agent Wendy Rodgers

Wendy Rodgers is the owner of Planet Realty & Management out of Jacksonville, Florida. Wendy specializes in working with investors and understands their unique needs very well because she's actually one herself. She started building her own portfolio in 2001, when she bought foreclosed homes that were not in great shape. She rehabbed them and then she either rented or sold them. She's also been featured on the cover of Top Agent Magazine.

What led you to real estate? Was it something you always knew you wanted to do?

I would say I stumbled into it. It started when I purchased my first home. I purchased a home that needed some work. I realized that with a little bit of elbow grease and hard work, you can increase the value, and therefore, build your equity in a home, which in turn, builds your fortune and what you can collect as far as going towards retirement, purchasing another home, and building up a portfolio.

What personal attributes, traits, or qualities have most contributed to your success? How did you develop these?

My best quality I have is my work ethic. I'm a high-energy person. I get up every morning with something to do. Having the drive and high energy makes it so that I can multi-task and get things done, keep pushing through even when I come across things that are setbacks.

How did I develop these? At a very young age, I had to support myself. If I did not work, I did not eat. I think that this pushed me towards being a successful, hardworking person.

Can you give specific examples of when these traits have played a role in your path toward success?

I definitely think so. During the crash of the market in 2006, when everything was going wrong, a lot of people gave up. I didn't give up. I kept pushing forward. I was a real estate agent at that point in time and I went on and got my broker's license so I could multitask and do several different types of jobs in the real estate market. I went into property management, into sales. I didn't have to share any of my commissions or bonuses with other real estate brokers. That's what drove me to open Planet Realty.

I always had a tough time splitting it because the real estate agent does do all the work. The broker collects a portion of it. Unfortunately, the bigger the company is, the more the money they take. I decided I was going to go out and do it on my own, which I can't say was easy. But if you push forward, you can make anything happen. That's how I see things in my eyes.

What were some of the major adversities and trials you had to overcome to achieve your goals?

A lot of things you have to overcome is learning to work with all different skill types, all different styles of houses and people, meshing, and being able to go with the flow. Sometimes a business can be unforgiving. You have to stand up, be the entrepreneur, be the leader, and learn how to work with things.

What kept you going despite these obstacles? Why didn't you give up?

I think a lot of it comes down to success. I came from pretty slim beginnings. I've made a pretty good name for myself here in Jacksonville. I live in the Neptune Beach area, near the beaches. Once you start becoming successful, you go to one thing and you accomplish something and then you go to another accomplishment. You start realizing the harder you push forward, the more success you have and the better person you become.

What is your vision for your career for the next five years?

During the next five years I'm really focusing on growth. I've always been very hands-on. I am out in the field every day. I am a real estate broker, but I don't take advantage of my real estate agents. I take them in and mentor them. I want to grow my business in several different ways. I would like to increase in terms of having more real estate agents. With the real estate agents I have, I mentor and I make sure that they feel that they're on the same level as I am. I also want to build in sales. Sales are pretty strong and the market has recovered tremendously. With that, if you build those things with property management, sales, and realtors, when the market does decline a bit (it is cyclical), hopefully there will be stability.

What do you feel is the best way you market yourself as a real estate professional for continual growth?

The best way I feel I can market myself and have growth is definitely by being a part of the community and volunteering. I try to give back to the community. Growth in terms of keeping everyone happy, building with real estate agents, building with sales, and keeping good customer relationships. People talk and people refer. One of the best things you can do for your business is have great relationships.

What's the biggest misconception/myth that people have about working with a real estate agent?

I believe a lot of people think real estate agents don't work, that real estate agents don't care, and that real estate agents make a lot of money without having to do much work. I think that's a big misconception because this is a very, very hard and competitive business. To keep your business going, you have to constantly be improving, moving, and creating good relationships with people. I think people really need to know that we really, really do work hard.

If you were to get a call from a family member in another state wanting to sell their home, what advice would you give them about selecting an agent who can best serve their needs?

I would actually do some research myself and determine the best company in that state. I would check their websites and Google reviews. Then I'd make some phone calls, talk to brokers and agents, and see how these agents are rated. There are different ways to refer, but I definitely would do some research before I just gave out a name, definitely.

The thing that comes up all the time is what is my house worth? You have to find an agent that's going to be honest and really tell you what your house is worth. Another one you get push-back on is what repairs need to be done to the house to get the price you want. How the house needs to be staged or what kind of upgrades you need in the house to sell the house for the price that you want.

How can someone who needs a real estate agent find out more about you and how you can help?

All they have to do is Google my name. Again, we're back to Google. You Google me, I come up at the top of the page. You can go to Planet Realty. I'm featured on realtor.com. You can also call me at (904) 425-SALE or 7253. I'm pretty easy to find.

RESOURCE SECTION

Top Loan Officer Marcia Gonzales

Marcia Gonzales of Home Street Bank, is based out of Vancouver, Washington. Marcia has been a loan officer for sixteen years. From 2006 to 2008 she was a certified mortgage planner. In 2013, she was named a five-star mortgage professional. In 2015, she was recognized as a top mortgage professional in Top Agent magazine. In 2013, she was a regular guest on the Hahn Show on KPDQ FM. She's currently a board member of Proud Ground, a nonprofit organization for first-time home buyers.

What led you to becoming a loan officer? Was it something you always knew you wanted to do?

Quite the contrary. A friend of mine was in real estate and he owned a real estate and mortgage company. He asked me for many years if I wanted to join his team and I said, "Oh, no way. Don't want to do it." Then he roped me into translating for a loan officer one time. As I was translating for the loan officer, the gentleman had asked me how much it cost to get started with the loan process. I asked the loan officer and she said nothing. I interpreted that and he said the last person he spoke with charged him $5,000, all of his money, and he didn't hear from them again. It just tugged at my heart. I spoke with my friend Norm and said, "Okay, I'm on board." Then I tried to see if I wanted to do the real estate or the mortgage side. I just liked working with numbers and I love working with people, so I chose to be a loan officer. From that point on, I've been hooked.

What personal attributes, traits, or qualities have most contributed to your success? How did you develop these?

I'm very persistent and driven and I don't give up on things. I treat each client with respect. I don't look at them as "just a loan" or "just money in my pocket." I try to cater my business to my clients and treat them like they're family. I say I'm tenacious, but my parents call it stubborn. Either way, it works.

Can you give a specific example of when these traits have played a role in your path toward success?

Like everybody, I've had adversities throughout my life. One my most recent ones was when I was in a serious car accident about two and a half years ago. It actually took me out of the business for about a year and a half. I continued to be persistent and tenacious and now I'm back full-time. I have pretty much picked up where I left off and I continue to grow my business with the same tenacity and drive.

What were some of the major adversities and trials you had to overcome to achieve your goals?

The perfect example would be the housing bubble. Everybody knows about that one, I'm sure. The whole industry felt it. If you've been in the business for any length of time you definitely felt it. I've been able to weather the storm and focus on the positive. This business is definitely not easy, even now. There have been so many recent changes in our industry that make it very difficult for loan officers, realtors, and borrowers, but I continue to stay focused and I don't allow things to discourage me. I just continue to persevere.

What kept you going despite these obstacles? Why didn't you give up?

My main driving force is my faith and my trust in God. That has helped me get through everything! What keeps me going and driven in this business are my clients. I love seeing the joy that they have when they buy a home or I'm able to help them lower their house payments. It's seeing them happy and being able to help others that make it all worth it.

In fact, I've helped a lot of first-time buyers, and when I tell them, "Okay, we have you approved for a home," they are shocked. They didn't think it was possible. Some have even cried. It's just a joy to see that and be a part of it.

What is your vision for your career for the next five years?

I made a decision to be on the board of Proud Ground, which is non-profit for first-time home buyers. I really want to make a positive impact in the community and continue to educate myself and to grow my business. I want to help make the "American dream" of owning a home possible, but not just owning the home. I also want to educate them. I see myself in this business for the next 30 years, until I retire.

What's the biggest misconception/myth that people have about working with a loan officer?

Unfortunately, I think it goes back to the housing bubble and that loan officers are greedy, that they don't care about their clients and all they care about is their bottom dollar. That's just not the case. We put a lot of long, hard hours in and we care about our clients. Yes, of course, the paycheck is good, but that's not our main focus nor should it be.

In what states are you licensed to assist people with home loans?

We lend in Arizona, California, Hawaii, Oregon, Washington, Idaho, Utah, and Alaska.

If someone was looking for a mortgage what advice would you give them about selecting a lender who can best serve their needs?

I think right now everybody is a rate shopper. Everybody is so concerned about rates and a lot of the time I show people that rates shouldn't be the main focus. When you're looking for a loan officer, ask more questions than just what the rates are. Ask them about the different loan programs they offer are, how you would beneift with a particular loan program. Look for somebody who's going to take the time to explain that to you and break things down so you understand why you're put into a certain program, why they chose a certain rate, and whether there are fees involved with that rate.

How can someone who needs a mortgage find out more about you and how you can help?

They can call my direct office number at 360-514-5958 or email me. My email address is Marcia.Gonzales@homestreet.com. You can also find me online at www.homestreet.com/mgonzales.

About The Author

"Believe you can and you're halfway there." —Theodore Roosevelt

Keith is the #1 Best-Selling Author of Publish to Profit (Available on Amazon), Host of Business Innovators Radio and Real Estate Innovators Radio, Founder of Authority Surge, and an honored husband, father, and grandfather.

Keith has over 24 years of progressive experience in sales and marketing. As a lead generation expert, Keith strives to implement the most cost-effective automated sales systems to bring new business in a streamlined manner to sustain continue business growth.

He effectively develops and implements targeted action plans to maximize productivity, efficiency, and profitability.

He has an exceptional ability to research and evaluate industry trends and competitor products and use the findings when designing and executing innovative strategies to boost company leveraging.

To reach Keith you can contact him via email at keith.dougherty@gmail.com.

If you are a real estate professional, as in an agent, broker, broker associate, mortgage broker; a home inspector; an appraiser; a real estate lawyer; a title company; or any professional in real estate and you would like to apply to be on our show, you can apply at our website: RealEstateInnovatorsRadio.com

Please be patient as our guess list has grown significantly.

Made in the USA
Charleston, SC
23 May 2016